To Kathleen

- those crazy crazy
days -

will we ever forget -

xx

WE
DIE
AT
DAWN

WE
DIE
AT
DAWN

*The true to life story
of America's NO. 1
radio team, or NO. 2,
or NO. 3,* KLAVAN *and* FINCH

by

GENE KLAVAN

DOUBLEDAY & COMPANY, INC.,
GARDEN CITY, NEW YORK, 1964

Library of Congress Catalog Card Number 64–11378
Copyright © 1964 by Gene Klavan
All Rights Reserved
Printed in the United States of America
First Edition

To

PHYLLIS,

without whose help.

A Table of Contents

FORWARD

by Senator Barry Goldwater

"Backward . . ."

—Barry

ACKNOWLEDGMENTS

It was obvious from the start that two people—especially a team of entertainers—were not going to write any book. Perhaps two people working as *associates* might write a book. Married people can write a book. Pairs of sociologists or psychiatrists write books. But with a comedy team, there can never be the necessary objectivity, the real prospect of fulfilling a mutual vision, or, let's face it, the work.

We tried. Lord knows, we tried. We sat together reminiscing, discussing, even drinking, anything to get the thing down on paper. All we ever arrived at was a late hour, a few more ideas for routines for the next show, and heads that hurt in the morning.

Finally, Dee Finch arrived at what he thought was the perfect solution.

"Gene," he said, *"You* write the book."

I frowned.

"You've written a few things; you like to putter."

I brightened.

"I don't have time for minor endeavors," he said.

And so are such things decided. Finch, however, cannot be held entirely free of responsibility. He felt impelled, as I sat writing, to criticize, censor, taunt, scoff, revile, mock, jeer, blaspheme, discredit. On occasion, he would even attempt to discourage me. At one point, he ventured the opinion that I could not write. Therefore, you will actually get some encompassment of our similitude and togetherness.

We would also like to blame George Hecht, a vice-president of Doubleday, Sam Vaughan, a senior editor of Doubleday, and Nelson Doubleday, a Doubleday of Doubleday, without whose blandishments, endearments, and offers of money this never would have happened.

—G.K.

CHAPTER 1

Teams Are Made and Then Borne

If you never write a book, there is a good possibility that no one will find out the truth about you. But if you do not write a book, there is also the possibility that no one will ever find out about you at all. Today, *everyone* is writing books, even authors. We have been a team in radio for eleven years and no one has found out about us yet. So we have nothing to lose.

You may have been under the impression that radio went out with the introduction of teenagers and violence to television. But radio will go on. Not only is it a superb medium, but it has a distinct competitive edge over television. It has long been known that television contains harmful rays which gradually reduce the water content of the human body. This process continues until finally one day, almost without your knowing it, your entire physical being pulverizes and you end up a small pile of sand on the floor. Perhaps some of the friends you have lost track of have already come to such a gritty end. Although we work for a company which owns and operates television stations, we urge you to forswear television and find other light to read by. TV is bad for you.

Our present company excepted.

Our real names are Gene Klavan and Dee Finch. Well, all right, L. Durwood Finch and Eugene Klavan. Perhaps we should have changed them, but, oddly, everybody thinks we already have. We are heard, as of publication date, on WNEW, a radio station often suspected of being the outstanding station in America. It is located close to Grand Central Station and the two are often confused. Especially the radio station. Since about November 1952 (we would have to look at the contracts) we have been able to comment on our fellow man with diabolical anonymity. We can say what we will about anybody or anything, virtually without limit, and then leave the studios free and clear, secure in the knowledge that no one who has heard us knows what we look like—or could possibly believe that we look the way we do.

Radio makes for invisible men. Perhaps, then, our readers might desire information about our physical characteristics. Combined, we stand eleven feet, nine inches tall and weigh 340 pounds. This is a considerable load, inasmuch as each member of the team thinks that he is carrying the other. There are two religions and two political parties which we switch from time to time. There are two wives, whom we do not switch, and six children who think everybody's father works in radio. Financially, there is one salary, which makes payday something of a scramble. If it were not for prior payroll deductions it is questionable that our mutual Uncle, Sam, would ever get his share.

We appear on the radio every morning live from 6 to 10 A.M., broadcasting to metropolitan New York, a luckless area of 15 million souls. In order to be on the air at 6 A.M., we must rise at 4:30 A.M. But fret not for us. A New York sunrise is quite possibly the most beautiful event ever seen by man. Unless you have seen a New York sunset, which is, the same thing in reverse.

People ask if we ever get accustomed to rising at 4:30 A.M. The answer is: never. Do we like it? We hate it. Why, then, do we do it? Frankly, neither man trusts the other; each is afraid that the other man will sneak in and take over the show.

If, since October or November of 1952 (we would have to look at the contracts), we have been living this blissful and largely anonymous existence why did we risk exposure with a chapter or two about ourselves? Primarily because the publishers have had a chance to read the rest of the manuscript and they have assured us that our anonymity is in no immediate danger. And, incidentally, *they* now want to look at the contracts.

Klavan and Finch, through attrition, is the end result of several successful and successive radio teams. Originally, the team consisted of two people known as "Jack and Gene." They were Jack Lescoulie and Gene Rayburn. After about a year and a half, Dee Finch replaced Jack Lescoulie. The team then became Rayburn and Finch and functioned happily for about five years. Then the span of that team ran out.

Teams do that. One will run along for years without incident or even a serious temptation to split and then eventually a discussion or a difference of opinion over show business, over each other's wives, over other people's wives, over billing or over an offer, dissolves it. But we have never had a single, serious difference of opinion, depending on your definition of serious.

I joined Finch in 1952 and we have remained through fat and lean, man and boy, for lo these many years. The main reason that Klavan and Finch have stayed together is that we had no differences of opinion. In fact we have no opinions whatever. The team is steady and secure. We remain under contract to ever wealthy WNEW until or unless WNEW decides to relinquish our services. (Thanks to an unusually generous and equitable contract—you should look at it—worked out for us by our attorneys, the noted Hershkowitz and Epstein, defenders of Billie Sol Estes and supporters of unpopular causes, we could be unemployed in fifteen minutes.)

People all over the United States, but especially Washington, want to know how this all came about—the team, I mean. To respond factually, the story begins in the late summer of 1952, when I left Washington, D.C., where I had been working in radio and television and proceeded to New York, where I was to make final contractual arrangements with television station WPIX. I had been urged by mutual friends to visit a "Dee Finch" who was seeking a replacement for his partner.

Now, to be fair, versions of this story differ a trifle. In the first place, I thought that the whole thing was a joke because of the improbability of anyone calling a grown man Dee Finch. But since truth, like justice, beauty, and contact lenses, is in the eye of the beholder, giving both sides of the story seem to be in order:

KLAVAN VERSION

I had heard about Dee Finch; in fact I actually had heard the team on CBS in 1952. I knew then that they were headed for disaster. I shall never forget the terrified look on Finch's face as he strode out to greet me in the lobby of that radio station in New York. Stark, clutching terror was in his eyes as he saw the one man who could save that cushy job WNEW dangled in front of him.

"KLAVAN! KLAVAN!" Finch shouted with tears in his shifty eyes. What could he say but repeat that magic name over and over? He begged me to come in for an audition to prove that, given the best support in the

FINCH VERSION

Klavan's name was given to me by a newsman friend of mine from Washington who told me that the kid had a raw talent of a minor league sort. He begged me to help the youngster because Klavan was on the verge of a crack-up—unable to get anywhere. He intimated that, if nothing else, the boy could take orders. I could mold whatever small talent he had into some assistance on the show which I had already made a living legend.

I'll never forget that small-town kid that I saw in that lobby that day. Dressed poorly, in the worst possible taste, he was downcast and full of doubt. I merely told nation, he could still carry on.

"There, there," I said, "get off your knees, people are looking. Try to be a man. Big Gene is here; all's right with the world." Under my tutelage, Finch blossomed in the audition and roared to new heights to which he had never aspired before. No longer was he just another anchor man on a comedy/selling team. He was somebody.

him to follow my lead in the audition I had arranged. His eyes were red and full of the tears of gratitude— but deep within there was evident fear. I guided him, kept him away from the executive vultures until I could shape him to what I wanted.

With me, I assured him, there were no heights he could not attain. He listened, I might say better than he does today, and he worked out all right. He was finally somebody.

I suppose we'll never really know so that the archives of art in this country will remain incomplete. In any case, we did become a team.

In that melange known as the entertainment world, teams are an uncommon commodity. Probably because producers, sponsors, networks have to contend with twice as much temperament, nearly twice as much in the way of studio facilities, and most important, have to pay twice as much to fill up the same amount of time.

We need not argue the merits of the diversification of

talent that two performers can provide. On second thought, maybe we *had* better argue the merits; you might have heard us on the radio.

Without the prejudice of fact to interfere with the lucidity of our thinking, it is easy to speculate on why it is that teams do not last forever. For one thing, I suppose, few people last forever. For another thing, I wish I had not said the other thing.

Undoubtedly the best team of our generation—assuming we are all contemporaries—was Dean Martin and Jerry Lewis. (Laurel and Hardy, Clark and McCullough, Smith and Dale, Neiman and Marcus, Plato and Socrates were all good but a little before my time.) There are other fine teams now, Wayne and Schuster, for example, and Bob and Ray, but they have never achieved the status of Martin and Lewis. If I have omitted any other team that you may enjoy, I hope you will understand that it simply is a manifestation of a subconscious hatred and jealousy. Nothing serious.

The essence of a good team is conflict. The attributes that make a team interesting, or hilarious, or at least better than run of the mill, are the sparks flying between the members of the team as they go about their funny business of being funny.

Martin and Lewis were a prime example of conflict; they were, in fact, almost an animated textbook on how to run a good team. The conflicts of their personal lives have nothing to do with the case—their roles as performers were one tangled mass of entertaining contradictions. Martin was smooth and phlegmatic, cool-headed, and sexy. Lewis was rough-edged, lost, childish, flamboyant, insane or inane. Together they were brash but lovable, inescapable, cute, at odds with each other but always a team. Each has since proven that he alone can be a productive performer but this, again, has little or nothing to do with their team appeal.

With Stan Laurel and Oliver Hardy, whose rather eerie return through television has endeared them to the nation anew, and introduced them to the whole nation of young people, it was a similar although not identical situation. The fat one, Hardy, felt that he was ever-capable, always in command, thoroughly indoctrinated in the technology of whatever situation was presented. Simultaneously, he was dogged by the troublesome, crying, lost little Laurel. The almost childlike antics of the skinny Laurel, lost in the convolutions of a world too complex for him, in the end managed to drag Hardy down into the mire, or in front of the car, or off a pier, or into jail along with his bewildered side-kick. On the surface, as we saw them, all was conflict. Although there were moments of real endearment between the two, their hold on the audience was endearing at all times.

The interesting thing is that in the Martin and Lewis combination, and in the Laurel and Hardy team, there wasn't a straight man in the bunch. Thereby we hang the point of this tale. Neither Klavan nor Finch is really a straight man. (It may be argued that neither of us is funny, either, but for anyone so tempted, please refrain. We depress easily.) Finch is steeped in the notion that he is a bastion of strength, supporting the whole team. Naturally, I maintain that the old bastion is incorrect; he should be sued for non-support. Further, he feels that he must anchor me because I am frequently capable of going off half-cocked. He thoroughly understands the exquisite technique of shooting me down off the ceiling if I have soared too high or pitched the pace too fast, according to him. Again he is incorrect. Little does he understand that it is *I* who am the marksman, that I have to pull in *his* horns, every once in a while, when he goes off on an editorial tirade on the air against the rights of women, or the indefatigability and the corruptibility of the Bureau of Internal Revenue. He has to be stopped before he destroys himself in the industry, can't he see that?

As a team, Klavan and Finch are saturated in personal conflict. We work in a soundproofed room about 30 by 30 feet. There are microphones, three turntables—we play our own records—and a control room which peeks down into our studio. The exit door is invariably left open because we suffer from a rare form of claustrophobia—it combines the fear of being in with the fear of being left out. The team likes the door open because you never can tell when something important might happen in the hallway outside, like a fight or a strike or a girl. We stand for the entire four hours as we work. This may be unique in the broadcasting business, but we are certain that we have been able to stand for more of our broadcasts than anyone else.

When the ON AIR light flashes on, it sometimes seems that we are able to read each other's mind, a trick which gives us precision in our dialogue if nothing else. But it is when the music begins, or a transcribed commercial starts that the real program commences. The studio roars with arguments over the correct pronunciation of Iago, the correct measurements of Sophia Loren, or the best method to eliminate crabgrass. On the basis of the latter argument, we came close to going our separate ways.

Then when the mike goes on, and we are supposed to blend our efforts to resume giving the public its entertainment and service, we stand looking daggers at each other, secretly hoping that the floor will open and swallow the other up. Since this is a financial marriage, however, we soon kiss our money and make up.

One of the by-products of this carrying on is the matter of language. It is embarrassing but necessary to admit that some of our invectives are words which we learned while serving with His Majesty's forces during the late war. It is worth a minute to talk here about dirty words. You know darn well, pardon the expression, that most people have a goodly supply of nasty words on which to call when the situation demands. When you work on radio or television, you cannot use the racy words when you need them. (What is worse, on TV you cannot even scratch.) Performers therefore have an excellent opportunity to discipline themselves to refrain from using *that* kind of talk forever. As a mere matter of precaution, it would seem that people who perform on the air, should never use language that ain't fit for Sunday-go-to-meetin'. In actuality, performers use more racy words off-mike than they might ordinarily, just as a release.

Even performers who are good family men, of fine

breeding, and a high cultural attainment, splendid physiques and an unlimited capacity for service, like ourselves, occasionally say rotten things that bounce out into the hall.

And because it only takes one ———— or a ————! to put you right out of broadcasting, one develops a kind of a habit of looking over the shoulder to see whether the ON AIR light is on. After years of this, our posture is peculiar, but at least we're safe.

Admittedly, we do come out at times with material that seems a trifle "blue," as they say in show business.[1] Let me assure you it is unintentional. Now and then one of us will say something that the other realizes is risqué, and the big thing at the moment becomes to continue, not to "break-up"[2] because laughing would be a giveaway. So if Finch gives voice to a *double-entendre*, I run away beyond the range of the microphone and double up laughing. It is his job to continue without giving evidence of the fact that he knows he has committed a nasty. Finch has an unpalatable trick which reverses the situation. If I am forced to do a little serious selling on the air, he is apt to get just far enough away from the microphone to be unheard and then mutter incantations and little unprintable funnies which he knows will put me into a giddy mood and ruin the whole commercial. And so it goes from cancellation to cancellation.

I always remember the terrifying experience of my early

[1] The words "blue material" came from the use of blue pencil to edit out objectionable material.
[2] The words "break-up" came from the use of blue pencil to edit out objectionable material. Or from someplace else.

days at a Baltimore (that may look like a dirty word, but it isn't) radio station. At that radio station, which shall remain nameless and therefore blameless, I once told a joke that I had heard, believing in my naïveté that it was a "shaggy-dog story." Unfortunately, it was not only shaggy, but dirty. Happy-go-lucky, and stupidly, I told it on the air.

The fascinating thing is that no one called up to protest or even wish me well in whatever kind of business I would have to enter. No one called at all. The significance of this, I have decided, is that either we had no listeners, or everyone was afraid to protest because it would have indicated that his mind was dirty, too.

There's no point in coaxing; I will not repeat the story here. The punch line, if it is of any consolation, was, "'Well,' said the farmer, 'if you're sure you won't be uncomfortable.'"

There is no question in either of our minds about the need for good taste. You cannot broadcast with the theory that what you can get away with is acceptable. Remarks which might be acceptable in casual conversation or in party groups are not acceptable to the same people listening to the radio, or watching TV. The question then becomes: Is the accepted acceptability acceptable?

There is one factor in our relationship which amazes us. We have an unwritten rule that we never discuss the program off the air. From six in the morning until ten, we deliver commercials, introduce records, dissect the station, improve the government, castigate the wrongdoers, and do our best to obliterate each other. But once the ten o'clock beep sounds, signifying the end of our broadcast day, we forget the program in conversation with each other. We never say "That was a good one!" We never mention what might be done to improve the show or what is good about it consistently.

The routines we do on the air are planned only insofar as I announce to Finch in advance that "I am a lighting technician for *My Fair Lady*," or his declaration that "You're a Communist." The ensuing routine has only the opener to work on. And, of course, it often sounds like it. When we have arrived at a line which seems about as funny as we think we are going to get, we bring in a record quickly, or some kind of run-off music, and hope that everyone in our listening area thinks as highly of us as we think of ourselves. It's a risky business, come to think of it.

Whenever we meet someone who says he listens, we always feel that the best technique is to say "thank you" regardless of whether he says he enjoys the program or not.

If he says he enjoyed us, we are thrilled. If he says he hates us, it is obvious that he just happened to hear us on one of his bad days.

The most unsettling thing about a critical encounter is that the critical person has a perfect right to say whatever he pleases, because when you start out to be a performer, no matter what kind, you're asking for it. And, in the words of that great American, John Dillinger, "You're gonna get it." Or, in the roar of M-G-M, *"Ars gratia artis."*

2

We Die at Dawn

For ten years or more, we have been getting up with more women than anyone else in New York. Ladies tell us this all the time. "I get up with you every morning," they say with a leer. And we, properly flustered, usually make a response, "The hell you say" and "Don't tell your husband" being among the most common.

Men, on the other hand, have a way of phrasing it more succinctly. "Jeeze, you jerks wake me up every day," they tell us reproachfully.

It is true that if you ever awake in the AM in New York City, or the commutable portions of New Jersey, Connecticut, Westchester, Long Island, or Pennsylvania, it is possible that you may find us talking to you. Our job is to wake you up, get you out, and sell you—anything and everything we can. If we can persuade you to buy one bottle of beer, one package of cigarettes, one automobile, one airline, one bowl of cereal, one loaf of bread more than you might have otherwise, we shall have done our job. The truth is, of course, that we don't really care if we sell you anything except ourselves. Someday, we think, taking the philosophical attitude, if you listen long enough, you will buy one or another of the things we are selling, simply out of curiosity, hate, revenge, amusement, or for escape.

If it's any consolation, we sell only quality products or services and we have two criteria to determine quality: (1) the goods and services must be good and serviceable (2) the sponsor must be able to pay the radio station. In extreme cases, we have been known to make a few concessions, especially in (1).

The show goes on the air at 6 A.M. Monday through Saturday. We go off the air, with a collective sigh of relief which can be heard all over the New York area, at 10 A.M. Except for an occasional day, we work those six days a week "live." The only days that we are tape recorded are those when we have been granted time off—to appear at benefits, sales meetings, or to conduct clandestine affairs. Many mornings we report to work in fragments, because of a sponsor's overzealous efforts in partying the night before. We never start any of this partying, mind you; we're just victims of circumstances. You know how it is when a client says, "Just one more, fellas." And you wives have heard this song before.

I seem to find the studios on time more often than Finch does. But then I am the junior man. Also, Finch is not quite as able to manipulate the streets of New York on hands and knees as adroitly as a younger man.

Frequently, we are asked why we do not do the program from home. We are asked, in fact, now and then, why we do the program at all. But the answer to the first question is that we are home too much now. One month of doing the program from home and we would have no homes at all.

There is another point of agreement between us: we share, oddly enough, the complete conviction that we have to come into the station. By going through the same discomfiting routines every morning that our audience experiences, we have an appreciation of their problems. We know what it is to get out of a warm bed—actually out of two warm beds—and wend our weary way to a job, every day in the week except Sunday, and including Christmas, Labor Day, Fourth of July, and Groundhog Day.

Does one ever get used to getting up at 4:30 A.M.? No. You do not. Never.

You also never get used to the idea of going to bed before the older children.

And on Sundays, when you can sleep, you can't sleep. But Lord knows, we do love our work passionately and we are not complaining.[1]

Once we get to the studios on Fifth Avenue, about three blocks from Radio City, we are locked into a little room and we get to work. The program has what we call a producer. This man, Mike Apicella, is more than merely a producer. He is runner, father confessor, liaison man with the executive staff of the station, and buffer against irate listeners and gnawing record pluggers.

Mike Apicella has been the producer for about ten years and, you might ask, what has he produced? We rise at

[1] One never knows who may read this book.

4:30 but Mike, as the producer, has to get up at 2:30. That's producing. He must get to the studio in time to get the real work done—producing the records, the commercials, and the like. Consequently, because of the tremendous job this man does, we find the studio setup, ready to go, the only thing missing being the trifling talent that we bring to bear on the program. Actually, we add a great deal.[2]

Mike Apicella is a man in his forties, or perhaps his sixties, with a frightening resemblance to Theodore Roosevelt, of sainted memory. Unlike that other great American, Mike speaks loosely and carries a big head. In all fairness to this man behind the scenes, if we allowed him in front of the microphone, he would undoubtedly be so good that the station would hire him and make us get up at 2:30 to pull the records.[3]

If by remote chance you have never heard our radio program, or if by remote chance you live some place other than New York, a brief description of the show would seem to be in order. The Klavan and Finch program consists of four hours of droll tomfoolery, interspersed with wildly humorous asides, brilliantly chosen recorded music, and scads of genuinely helpful information for the waking hours. It is full of good cheer, big laughs, and happiness. If you *have* heard the program, then you know that what we say is true; it does take four hours.

Finch plays the part of an interrogator for any number of make-believe people that I bring in, through sound

[2] The same one might be reading this page.
[3] At least he says he gets up at 2:30—but who would check?

effect doors or windows. The number of characters produced on any single day is limited only by our imagination, inclinations, or hangover. I seem to have the facility for doing numerous acents and dialects and characterizations and I am assured that they sound exactly like the person I intend them to sound like. Finch, in corroboration, thinks every one of them sounds like me.

Since the entire program is ad-lib—that is without any written material whatsoever (the phrase is from the Latin) —at times the bits come off and at times they should never have gone on. The redeeming and wonderful thing is that we don't remember what we say as soon as we have said it. You have heard of people with total recall? Well, we have total forget.

Another admirable feature about our work, we are agreed, is that we do not use other people's material. Other people are agreed too. But the total inanity is our own. If we are lousy, we have no one to blame but ourselves. If we are good, everyone thinks we have writers. However, this can easily be disproven. If we had writers, the truth would soon be out. We don't read too well.

Further, if we start a routine, and it is getting nowhere —if, as we say in the jargon of the trade, it is dying and taking us with it—we say so. Our public would much rather have us abandon it in midstream than force them to choke on their coffee, or take their hands off the wheels to switch dials.

If we are bad, we know it as soon and perhaps a little before the listeners and we beat them to it by announcing that we are dying, Egypt.

We have one other element that few programs, comedy or straight, can match. Timeliness. We can comment or do a routine on something that has just been announced during a newscast because we ad-lib. And by phony electronics, we can invite imaginary guests from Teheran, Cuba, Washington, or even New York. The President's cabinet or Russia's commissars are only one doctored microphone away.

At times we are satirical, at times downright nasty, and occasionally, by report, funny. But the peculiar thing is that we are enjoying ourselves and that is saying a good deal in these days of messy roll-on deodorants and frozen cookie dough.

During the course of the program, we eat breakfast, shave, greet the arriving employees of the studios. We share our morning with the listener, even though he didn't ask, gripe about the weather, exult about the exultable, mutter about the mutterable, and comment on events that need it, like the World Series, the mayoralty election, gasoline taxes, stolen shopping carts, or Brigitte Bardot. We insult our boss because we have a contract, feel free to insult our wives because they don't listen, and plug our dentists and physicians because they cannot advertise and they hurt us with drills and needles.

Finally, when the great hour comes and it is 10 A.M., we advise the audience to turn the radio off. Nothing, but nothing, could follow us. In truth, we are afraid that if people continue to listen, they could hear a number of the good things on the station and that would ruin it for us.

After ten, we rush to our office, being careful not to

knock over the mops or soap buckets or paint cans, to answer the occasional letter that finds its way there. Then we are free to lunch with our sponsors or advertising agencies.

It is surprising how much of this contact work is involved in our careers. But since we have a roster of over fifty clients each morning, it seems only fair that we get a chance to meet with these people and come to understand their problems. Actually, this is an impossible task because to begin with, we do not even understand our own problems.

One of the most fortuitous qualities of our work is that neither of us should ever have to seek psychoanalysis. The reason is simple: we get to say everything that is on our minds every morning. And if it sounds crazy enough, we get a raise.

CHAPTER 3

The Business Lunch

The most frequent consolation people offer us for the strange way of life we lead, and especially the hours we keep, is that we are lucky fellows to be able to go home at about ten o'clock in the morning. Nothing could be further from the truth.

Maybe there are some things further from the truth, but that seems irrelevant. Actually, 10 A.M. is frequently the start of our working day. At least the hardest part of it. We spend at least three days a week at business luncheons.

This makes a certain amount of sense. After all, if you hire someone to do your commercial, pay for time, you would like the announcer and the people at the station to know as much as possible about your product. The more the announcer knows, the more he can say. And in the case of a couple of clowns, the more they can say, the longer the one-minute commercial they can do about it. The business lunch is the place where such matters are discussed and such vital information promulgated.

It is quite clear that the bread and butter of American free enterprise today is food and drink. As a matter of stark, authentic fact, most business worth the name in the

United States is transacted at luncheon. The business meeting, conference, the ordinary consultation have been virtually eliminated. Everything has been replaced by lunch except dinner. And dinner has been replaced, for most of us, by low-cholesterol, salt-free diets, and Alka-Seltzer.

These days, American industry gets down to the business at hand through the mouth. This produces what is known as routine, hand-to-mouth business. When you have made the rounds, as we have, for years, it seems curious that one of the problems continually facing our government is the food surplus.

The business luncheon is so much matter of standard procedure that recently, when we learned of a major calamity in the office of one of our advertisers, there seemed little at which to be surprised. It began when the vice-president in charge of sales at Woolhair Linens, Inc. (the name has been changed to ensure the renewal of their account) received a letter from a customer which caused a stir.

The executive, whose name oddly enough was A. Saleschief, read the letter aloud, then clapped his hand to his forehead. The buying staff of Monkscloth Shirts, a major Woolhair account, wrote that they would like to cancel a scheduled luncheon in favor of a meeting in Saleschief's office.

Mr. Saleschief, a successful young man of forty—all men who are successful are young at forty—called his assistant immediately. The assistant entered.

"Furst," demanded Mr. Saleschief, "did you see this letter? Monkscloth has canceled the luncheon!"

"No sir, Chief, but I think we have an open Wednesday between the twenty-first and the twenty-fifth of the month, and open dates at Twenty One and the Stork Club," Mr. Furst replied with the true efficiency of a born follower. Furst, being less successful, was old at forty-five years of age.

"I don't think you understand, Furst—they're not rescheduling the luncheon, they're coming *here*. What could it mean? Has anything like this ever happened before?"

Furst became pensive. "I don't think so, sir. Of course, I've only been here since the '57 cleanout. It seems to me we might have had a meeting in the office a few months before the '58 shake-up, or maybe it was right after the late '59 reorganization. It seems improbable, though. The Monkscloth people are from Philadelphia. No one ever comes to New York from Philadelphia without coming for lunch."

Both men stared at each other.

"Perhaps," Furst said, "they're trying to catch us off guard."

"That's what it is," Mr. Saleschief said triumphantly. "Our competitors are taking them to lunch."

Furst was furious. "I can't believe that, sir. We take them to the best places: Eden Roc, Pierre's, Giovanni's, the Four Seasons. We've toasted them in the biggest bars of the big town. Why, we've given them the best cheers of our lives!"

Both men laughed companionably, breaking the tension.

"Nevertheless, whereas and notwithstanding, they're

coming on up here. Here, to the Home Office." Saleschief was inconsolable again.

"What'll we do with them?" Furst asked, with just a note of hysteria creeping into his normally well-pressed voice. He continued, after receiving no answer, but was unable to forestall a rising pitch: "Where could we have a meeting?"

"Ha!" Saleschief said, "I've got it—how about the meeting room?"

"Sir, you know perfectly well that the girls have their French lessons and coffee breaks in there. It's one of their fringe benefits," Furst pointed out.

Saleschief, rebuffed, leaned back in his leather swivel bucket seat, puffing on his cigar and mentally executing labor leaders. He was out of original ideas.

"We might use your office," Furst said tentatively.

"What?" boomed Saleschief. *"My* office? Do you think, you idiot, that I want a lot of strange customers walking around in here, tracking up my rug? It's bad enough that the damned staff has to come in here once a week."

"But sir," Furst said, trying to gain ground, "perhaps they could remove their shoes as we do when we come in." He held up his low-cut French calfskins to emphasize the point.

"No, damn it, no. Besides, I don't have nearly enough martini glasses. I only have enough for my secretary and myself. I keep an extra for the president, but he hasn't been in for four years."

"I guess you're right. Martinis are necessary."

"Necessary?" Saleschief wiped his brow with his $100

sleeve. "I've been doing business with Monkscloth for six years and I've never gotten beyond the weather in Philadelphia until I have had three martinis. I don't even recognize those men sober."

"You mean you sober or them sober?" Furst asked.

"Either."

"Then," Furst said, "we'll get martinis here somehow. Maybe the Forum has a takeout counter."

Suddenly, the face of the sales executive brightened. He looked at, or rather through, Furst.

"Get your assistant in here, Joe what's his name."

"You mean Segunda?" Furst said, in disbelief.

"Yes, get him in here. He's not high enough on the table of organization to go to our lunches. Maybe he'll have a glimmer on how to deal with this."

Furst could feel the hot breath of Segunda's promotion on the nape of his well-barbered neck. He tried to protest lightly, saying that Segunda was usually out of the office, wasting his time, making sales calls or something of the sort. But it was useless to try forestalling the inevitable. Saleschief demanded to see Segunda.

In a short time, Segunda arrived, held in a nearly invisible armlock by Furst. Segunda entered the office, looking around, in awe. He had been employed by the company shortly after receiving his Ph.D. at Harvard. Yet in his three years at Woolhair, he had never once been in this office. Any dealings he had with his superiors were always at lunch.

"The rug, the rug!" Furst whispered from the threshold. "Take off your shoes."

Segunda slipped out of his loafers and held them awkwardly in his hands. Then he advanced slowly, to stand enthralled before the richly ornamented desk of the vice-president.

"Segunda, we've got trouble," Saleschief said, "big trouble." He beckoned Segunda to be seated in the only other chair. Furst sat down cross-legged on the comfortable nap of the rug.

"Segunda, we're going to have a meeting here in the office with Monkscloth."

"You're kidding!" Segunda said, dropping his loafers.

"Damn it, I'm not kidding. Maybe you're a guy who can help us. You still see buyers in their places, don't you? You go into their offices and all? You still have buyers into your office, don't you?" Saleschief knew that he was placing himself squarely at the mercy of his underling, but the moment was desperate.

Segunda said nothing for a moment. He slipped back into his loafers. Then he reached over and took a cigar from his boss's humidor. He sat back ceremoniously and puffed a rich, full puff of smoke in Furst's direction.

"All the time," Segunda said, finally, removing the cigar to turn it in his fingers, gazing at it reflectively.

"Well, for the Lord's sake, what *do* you do when they're in your office? What do you do before you've had a drink and you don't have a filet to fool around with?" Saleschief was frantic.

"Well," Segunda said, as one would address a child, "are these men or women?"

"Men! Men, all men!"

"Well, then, first I invite them to sit down."

"Yes?"

"They sit down."

"Yes, yes—go on."

"Pretty soon I ask how the weather was in their part of the country when they left."

"All right, all right, what happens then?"

"They tell me." Segunda spoke slowly, savoring his comments.

"Yes, yes, then what?" asked the vice-president, sitting on the edge of his bucket seat.

"You're killing me—what do you do then?"

"Well," Segunda said, his composure slipping just a mite, "about that time I take out my credit cards and riffle through them. In a moment, I suggest a nice bar and grill for lunch."

The vice-president stood up to his full height. "Is that *all* you do in that goddam office?"

"It's a small office," Segunda said, choking on his cigar, "besides, the girls have to use it at one-thirty for their yoga sessions. It's one of their fringe benefits, you know."

"Take off those shoes!" Furst roared, from the floor.

CHAPTER 4

Hot Flashes

Before World War II, there were less than a thousand commercial broadcasting stations in the United States. Television stations were experiments, flickering around in one or two places in the country. *Life, Liberty, American,* and *Collier's* were part of our pursuit of happiness. Today, of those hallowed old names, only *Life* remains. This has its encouraging aspects, where there's *Life,* there's *Time.* I'm not so sure about *Fortune.*

Since the end of the Second World Unpleasantness, the nation has seen the burgeoning of thousands of radio and TV stations. Every one of these new stations has increased the demands on news gathering media because each of the stations presents some form of news. The competition for news has become almost insurmountable. Newspapers, radio, TV, magazines, wire services all have reporters moving about the scene, scrounging for the latest of the latest, the newest of the new.

A morning program, especially, must have the fresh news because it begins the day for many people. Consequently, Klavan and Finch must have an awareness of what is going on around us and what is likely to happen

in our timespan on the air. We work very closely with the
newsroom so that tragedy or pathos are not introduced by
comedy or bad taste. At least, I hope it comes out that
way. But the intensity of the competition for news has
forced onto the public a searchlight which often transcends
good taste and frequently strips from the people the common privilege of privacy which they should be allowed.
Let us give you an example of how this attempt to present
everything has effected the coverage of news.

A fire alarm sounds in the nighttime peace. Insidious,
ravenous flames lick and nip at an apartment house in a
pleasant middle-income neighborhood. Suddenly, the entire area is aware of the feel, the smell of tragedy. The
aura of danger and dread of the unconquerable engulfs
the community. One apartment dweller arrives home late
and at the same moment as Jack Flash, the radio reporter
and man-on-the-street. The apartment dweller, a small
man of forty-five, sees the smoke pouring from all sides of
the building. Shrugging off any consideration for his own
safety, he rushes toward the inferno. Jack Flash stops the
man as he is tearing his jacket into shreds to use as a smoke
mask.

"Hi, there, I'm Jack Flash of Radio Central. I wonder if
you would tell us your name, sir?" Jack has a small tape
recorder about the size of a camera. He points the highly
polished microphone at the resident's mouth.

"My wife, my family—they're in there!" the father and
husband shouts uncooperatively.

"Can you hold off that comment till we get your name,

sir? I'm sure our vast metropolitan audience would like to hear the sound of tragedy firsthand," Jack says engagingly above the sound of crashing glass.

"I've *got* to get to them!" the apartment dweller says, trying to sidestep Jack Flash and his shiny mike. But Jack, knowing his duty to the public, his obligation to keep them informed, throws a judo hold on the interviewee and flings him to the ground. Narrowly missing a falling armchair, Jack, helping the distraught chap back to his feet, is courtesy itself.

"Now sir, what were your exact thoughts when you stopped your car, got out and saw your home burning?" Jack asks politely.

"Don't jump! Don't jump!" the interviewee calls suddenly, pointing to the third floor.

"Surely, as you stepped from your car, saw the flames coming out of the window, some little observation creased your mind that you would like to tell our Action Central listeners." Jack turns to smile at the gathering neighbors who, with civic pride, are watching the interview. The crowd has, of course, seen fires before, but none of them has ever seen Jack Flash in person and they are justifiably proud that he has selected their neighborhood to visit with his famed roving microphone.

Now faced with the increasing number of competitive newsmen arriving, plus the rising tumult as the roof begins to collapse, Jack feels himself begin to tense slightly. As he holds the dweller in his iron grip, Jack realizes that he must contain himself.

"Is that your sports car blocking the hydrant?" a fireman asks Jack disrespectfully.

"I have a press card for God's sake," Jack says summarily, dismissing the shamefaced intruder. He is probably new to the force. The struggling resident suddenly pulls himself up for a massive effort. He shouts, "*AAAAEEEEI-IIIIIIIII!*" with a wild, open tone.

"Could you do that again? Dammit, I wasn't cued up," Jack says impatiently. "With a little consideration from you, I may be able to get a Peabody Award. See if you can approach the same key." Jack is proud of his earlier training as a music librarian.

The scene is a tableau, clogging now with impedimenta of modern broadcasting and reporting. Cameras and flash guns working like sparklers, whirring TV news cameras and newsreel machines add to the sound of chaos. One of the most famous of the tabloid newspaper photographers rushes over to Jack Flash and his captive interviewee shouting, "Lemme get him for a minute, Jack. Don't be such a hog!"

"He's mine, my exclusive," Jack responds defiantly.

"Gimme that expression again will you, mister!" another photographer shouts. "Now just one more, to be on the safe side," he continues. Jack holds the man firmly, afraid that the inconsiderate apartment dweller will defect to the representatives of the printed word.

"Oh my family, my family," the man murmurs, tears welling in his smoke-reddened eyes. The tabloid photographers and reporters ignore a crumbling wall for just one more shot of the man and his highly pictorial hysteria.

Pictures of firemen going after people in the midst of unspeakable horror have been done to death, so to speak. But a paper can always use a good head shot of a crying man for the front page or the centerfold.

"Look, mister, I've *got* to get something on this tape for my nine-thirty beeper phone," Jack urges enticingly. "Don't you want to hear yourself on the radio?" But before the fellow can even attempt compliance, a camera from a distinguished newspaper is forced in his face. Jack pauses long enough to place his head on the shoulder of the harassed citizen so that their picture may appear together in the famous newspaper if it is fit to print.

"My Lord, there they are!" the apartment dweller calls out, as he sees his family being safely evacuated to an awaiting ambulance. But before he can get to them, a burly fire chief shoulders his way into the deluge of reporters. The resident has escaped from Flash but is now caught tight between two pushing men.

"Chief, I say, Chief, how does it look to you?" This cogent question comes from Marvin Grommet, the well-groomed reporter for Press Management Associates, representing 350 radio and TV outlets in the U.S. and Canada.

"Get the hell out of my way," snaps the crusty old firehorse, pushing the microphone away from his nostrils.

"There they go, my wife, my children . . ." the small voice of the man says but his comment is all but engulfed in the huge mass of humanity viewing the scene.

"Would you say, Chief, that the department is understaffed?" Grommet asks, swiveling the mike back into the face of the overworked public servant.

The chief grasps the microphone and bows to the insistent searchlight of the free press. "I would say," the chief intones in a full, rich voice, "that the department needs an increased budget for the next fiscal year. More men, more equipment, are the answers to a greater service to the pub—"

Seizing this dramatic moment, the apartment dweller manages to wrench free and heads for the ambulance into which his family has disappeared. He drops down into a crawling position, and sneaks through the crowd of autograph seekers, to reach the safety of the waiting vehicle. Once inside, the ambulance roars away with accustomed efficiency.

The apartment dweller is safe in the arms of his family and he embraces each member in the fervor of a reunion snatched from horror and tragedy. Suddenly, he is aware that the ambulance is not approaching the hospital but a similar building, sterile and immense with a private entrance marked AMBULANCE ENTRANCE. The edifice is obviously not a hospital however.

"Hey," the father and husband calls out to the driver, "this isn't the hospital."

"I know that," says the driver of the rescue wagon, "this here is the television station. I get twenty bucks for every scoop I bring in. We're just in time for the nine-thirty news roundup."

CHAPTER 5

Payola and How It Grew

One of the disillusionments of modern-day America was the uncovering of the existence of payola in the broadcasting business. America was shocked to discover what filth and skulduggery lay behind the simple playing of records on the air. But the real tragedy was that the revelation cut off a lot of good men from a lot of good money.

We were disappointed when the findings came to light. Personally neither Klavan nor Finch ever took any payola. Not only because of our scruples, but because nobody offered us any. At least if we had been offered something to play records we would have had the security of feeling like *somebody*.

Going out and soliciting for payola is not really cricket. It's like any other kind of soliciting. But we feel that it was wrong to make payola a crime and a federal crime at that. When Congress legislated against payola, a little of the American Way died.

Actually, since payola has only recently come into our vernacular, the word itself probably deserves an explanation. Payola: a sort of bribe for playing a bad record for too long a time, too often; to indulge in payola, a table is customarily required—not a turntable—to slip the money under. However, until recently, according to some of the congressional findings, even the table was unnecessary. Until recently, payola was, you should excuse the expression, just one of those things.

Klavan and Finch having, unhappily, failed to receive any of the fruits of the payola harvest, it was peculiar, therefore, when the payola hearings started that people should stop us on the street, wink a nasty wink, nudge us in the tummy and ask, "How about that payola bit, eh Skippy?" It was a question much like "Have you stopped beating your wife?" What do you respond? As a matter of fact, how do you answer any question that begins with "How about that . . ." unless you're Mel Allen.[1] If you just dismiss the subject with a cursory "Yeah," you're guilty. If you start to give a detailed description of the whole business, a glazed look of disbelief comes over the eyes of the interrogator or he assumes a look of benign tolerance. So we adopted the simple policy of winking in return and saying "Shh!" It worked. But our children may have to be answered someday when they ask, "Why doesn't Daddy have any friends except Mr. Epstein, the lawyer?"

Don't think, dear reader, that you have heard the last of this payola business however. As an illustration, the drugstore we once used was operated by an able, intelligent entrepreneur; he was also, fortunately, a druggist. When the payola thing was at its screaming headline height, he opened all conversations with "Well, listen, you really can't

[1] Mel Allen, a well-known bachelor sportscaster, often says "How about that?"

blame a fella if he sees an opportunity to advance himself." Then he would quickly add: "If it doesn't hurt anybody, I mean." This little dialogue had the sound of pleasantry but, underneath, it was excoriating. We always felt that deep down inside he didn't even mean well.

It was not more than a month or so after the hearings on payola closed that the Congress decided to look into the drug business. They saw then what was going on in the way of unethical practices in that field. Although we did not have a cold or even need toothpaste, we made it a practice during the pharmaceutical hearings to drop by that drugstore daily to assure the druggist that you really couldn't blame anybody for trying to advance himself— if it didn't hurt anybody.

Now that the drug investigation is over, other investigations have been started. And there will be others until finally the whole rotten core of decadent America has been laid bare for all to see. Of course, the inquisitions could have been stopped if the people of this country had risen to the occasion and adopted the K and F plan for the future of this nation. We advocated formation of a nonpartisan committee of radio announcers to investigate Congress. Naturally, all of these disc jockeys would be citizens and several of them would have to be over twenty-five so as to be above the influence of the American teenager. Blindly, no one of import took this proposal seriously.

Lest we be taken facetiously, allow us to remind you: payola is the buyword in our country and has been for generations. Let us place before you a number of turgid questions which *have never been put forward* before because nobody has the kind of guts it takes to ask such questions:

Why is the capital of this country in Washington, D.C., and not in Philadelphia or New York where it started out? Who was the smart Maryland landowner who was stuck with that piece of property on the Potomac? He got to somebody.

Would Appomattox Courthouse have been selected as the surrender site of the Civil War if some clever public relations man hadn't slipped somebody something to keep a smart resort like Virginia Beach from becoming more famous?

How did Mrs. Lincoln manage to get last-minute tickets to that hit play *Our American Cousin?*

Were Gilbert and Sullivan *that* good?

Is David Merrick really David Susskind?

For that matter, the You Do Something for Me; I'll Do Something for You theory is part of the American grain. Congress spends half its time doing things for people who have done things for them. And how many presidential appointments go to people who helped? What about the venerated apple for the teacher?

Friends, don't let them stop payola. At least not completely. Christmas should be a time for joy and giving and receiving. Stop the practice of giving business gifts at Christmas and you rock the very foundations of the American economy. Our business society would topple like a melting gelatin mold, or some like simile.

For further discussion of payola, we will be glad to address ourselves to your requests. If you write, however, do

3

so in a plain, unmarked envelope. Just slip it under our studio door. Or if you are interested in personal discussion, in New York the number to call is YUkon 6-7000.

If we're not there, for Heaven's sake do not leave any messages.

CHAPTER 6

A Better Life Through Advertising

Surrounded as we are, all of us, by commercial announcements each day, it is a phenomenon that we have not actually changed our way of living. Come to think of it, that's the wrong way to begin this chapter because we *have* changed our way of life in this country as a direct result of the creative, ingenious radio/TV, newspaper, magazine, billboard, and direct mailing advertising. Of course, our way of life may have changed subtly but it is not equally true that we ourselves have changed. Not at heart. Nor have our maladies changed. We still suffer from the same evils that plagued our fathers and mothers—halitosis, gaposis, pimples, vitamin deficiencies, overexertion, undernourishment, tension, coffee nerves, and those washday blues.

The main reason we remain unchanged is because we do not live the way advertisers think we should. We don't act the way we are supposed to act, according to the dramatized messages, or say the things they want us to say.

This is all the more peculiar, for in America today we are constantly besieged with the vernacular of the advertiser. Day and night we are splattered with the hard, fast sell. Klavan and Finch, as broadcasters, are of course never guilty of this heinous wrong. We don't sell with the hard, fast sell because we are not hard or fast enough. But we do have transcribed and recorded messages on our show and *they* are hard and fast, so in a sense, to be candid, we do play fast and loose with the hard and fast.

We resist the radio and TV commercials because they purport to be stories of just average American households, conversations between husband and wife, conversations between lady neighbors, discussions with the children—anything that represents normal America at work or play. After the initial buildup, when the problem has been stated, when Jane tells Mary that she and Jim can't go to the party because she has a headache, when Mother tells little Joey that he has just messed up his bluejeans, when hubby comes home from the job feeling rundown, out jumps the voice of a convenient announcer who has the remedy. Yet is this real? Did you ever wonder where those unseen announcers have been all during the first part of the commercials? Sometimes I hate to go to work because that hidden announcer may be in my very home waiting to pop out of the breadbox.

The whole trouble, naturally, is that we don't yet talk and live the way they think we do on those commercials. If we did, this would be a happier nation. Husbands and wives would always have much to talk about and all remedies would be at hand.

To help rectify this problem we have written a script for you to follow in real life, and, as they say on the radio, here it is now:

HUSBAND: (*Entering kitchen, wet and tired, slops muddy, filthy feet on the shining linoleum*) Hi, Honey, I'm home! (*He puts his freshly shaved face next to her shining hairdo and almost kisses her.*) Oh, *gosh,* look what I've done, I've tracked mud all over your nice, clean floor!

WIFE: (*Smiling broadly, and brandishing filter-tip cigarette*) Don't worry, sweetheart, I can clean the dirt and grime in half the time, in fact in half a minute, I can clean the whole house and all that's in it.

HUSBAND: (*Taking hand to his lips—her hand—and kissing it through the pink lotion*) I *love* your soft, white hands but, (*wiping lotion from lips—his lips*) I think —pardon me for saying this, darling—but haven't you been smoking more now and enjoying it less?

WIFE: (*Downcast, pulls away*) It's only because—well, you know, crazy, busy me—it's just that I can't brush after every meal.

HUSBAND: You can't? Your nagging backache?

WIFE: No, your mother went home this afternoon. Now, no need to make excuses since her plates don't slip, she eats everything.

HUSBAND: She's gone by bus and left the driving to them, I hope. Tell me something about your mother: Does she or doesn't she?

WIFE: I think only her hairdresser knows, but now the makers of twenty-seven leading top-loading automatic washers include her detergent.

HUSBAND: Well, I'll send her flowers by wire, because then something warm, and human and wonderful happens.

For that matter, isn't there someone who's thinking of *you* tonight? A long distance call might set your mind at ease.

WIFE: (*To herself*) No, I've let romance fade, fade, fade away. I never carry on more than I can afford to.

HUSBAND: (*Looking around the house*) Say, sweetheart, where are our healthy, active, growing youngsters?

WIFE: They wanted to be the first on the block to own the new, all new—

HUSBAND: Well, their group did have fewer cavities . . .

WIFE: (*Shyly*) And they can't brush after every meal.

HUSBAND: But you shouldn't have sent them down to the friendly neighborhood merchant in this weather. Would you believe it, they'll have a cold?

WIFE: I'll do what doctors do for the aches and pains of cold or flu, I'll give them a combination of medically approved ingredients.

HUSBAND: Not aspirin alone, without antacids?

WIFE: So, I'll buffer 'em up a little.

HUSBAND: (*He walks to her and presses his fingers to her temples*) You're getting loggy and out of sorts. You can be sure if it's—

WIFE: Logey, dammit not loggy! And never mind that, why don't you take me out to the sun and fun country?

HUSBAND: I've got to watch my savings grow.

WIFE: We could go now and pay later.

HUSBAND: Listen, I was born in 1925, I've got to look forward to the golden years. Life's not just one big dream in your Maiden form.

WIFE: Well, I'm tired of apartment living, ready to own my own home, nothing down, years to pay.

HUSBAND: Turn on your favorite station for music and news, you'll feel good again.

WIFE: (*Becoming angry*) Oh, you—why you still use that greasy kids' stuff on your hair.

HUSBAND: Why don't you just take tea and see!

WIFE: (*Starting to sob*) You never care enough to send the . . . the very best!

HUSBAND: Why . . . you . . . you . . . you're full of polyunsaturated fat!

WIFE: (*Screaming through her tears*) You don't even think young!

HUSBAND: What do you know, you can't even sing along with Mitch. (*The wife, shrieking uncontrollably, rushes to medicine cabinet, pulls out a bottle of properly marked Brand Name prussic acid capsules and throws them at husband. He starts to dissolve.*)

WIFE: (*Watching him go*) Better things for better living through chemistry!

HUSBAND: Pain persists! (*Voice hardly audible*) Call a physician! (*Only a puddle remains*)

WIFE: Well, what do you know? He's gone. My headache's gone.

CHAPTER 7

Our Late Friends

Thanks to a brilliant job of internal organization in this book, you have learned about our professional life and like that. Now you are entitled to information about our home life. Doing a morning program, we have become two of the many thousands who rise early and go to bed early. Benjamin Franklin, of course, said that this makes you healthy, wealthy, and wise. But any guy who stands around in a thunderstorm holding a wire and a skate key cannot be all that smart.

The problems of our wives are quite different. Neither one gets up at the same time as her husband. Neither can go to bed at the same time. Of course, that is what we fought for—a better America, democracy for all, and the right of a wife to sleep until the children set her feet on fire.

Our outgoing social life is less of a problem than the stay-at-home evenings, but it still has its distinctive aspects. When we go out to dinner, for example, we go at 5:00 P.M. Inasmuch as New York is basically a nighttime town, we are usually served while the waiters are still complaining about the tips from lunch. We can get to the Broadway theater only for matinees and we see most movies at a time when no one else is able to sit still that long, or is playing hooky, or is out of work. The eccentricities of our work, however, have not impaired our enjoyment of the movies; the most important thing about any motion picture is to get there before the prices change.

The major problem centers around mid-week, at-home, social life. It has come to be all but non-existent. What kind of a life can you have when the host has to go to bed before the seven-year-old? How can you tell guests that if they do not leave soon, you will be in a coma by 6:15 A.M., at a time when you are supposed to be scintillating or at least broadcasting?

For an example of the sort of thing that happens after an evening at our homes, the following is a small taped segment of a broadcast done as we were both still trying to punch the sleep out of our eyes. This was a morning following an ordinary evening at our home, when we had a few friends in, say, perhaps, the Duke and Duchess of Windsor and the William Holdens.[1]

FINCH: It's 38 degrees and cloudy . . . Now, here's Klavan with a word from Tareytons.

KLAVAN: It's 38 degrees and cloudy.

FINCH: I said that.

KLAVAN: Oh. (*yawn*)

(*Here Finch does a 30 second commercial. It takes 4 minutes.*)

[1] Fictitious names are used throughout to prevent revealing the identity of our real friends, say, the Aristotle Onassises and the Elizabeth Taylors.

KLAVAN: 38 degrees and cloudy, and Finch—

FINCH: All right, old buddy, what's our next musical selection?

KLAVAN: It's a hot, new release called . . . Degrees and cloudy.

As you can see, our problem is complex. We have to keep clear minds for the daily battle of sponsors and ratings. We must keep alert in order to secure our already substantial lead over the thousands of mildly talented radio men, as well as those who walk in off the street seeking our jobs and who are better equipped.

Therefore, the problem is to get friends, close and otherwise, out of the house before the coffee is due or especially before the brandy appears. Brandy, as everyone knows, is a stimulant which will keep all hands alive and vivacious. At times, our wives try to help. But it can be extremely unpleasant for a grown man to hear his wife say, "All right, darling, now tell everybody good night, and go up to bed. There's a good boy." The thing to do, then, is to have occasional guests in during the week, but to develop a technique for making them understand that this is to be a brief but pleasant encounter. You can be putting the cat out as they come in, for example. Or leaving a note for the milkman. Finch has a system which sometimes works, but it takes a sense of humor on each side to carry it off. When he has tried his hand at subtleties, which fail, he then jumps up on the sofa and shouts, "Get out, damn it! Haven't you got a home?" This always leads to immediate laughter, especially when he says, "Get the hell out!" because Finch is known as such a great little kidder. Unhappily, he went too far on one occasion with this gimmick and finally fetched an old friend a clout and sent the poor chap sprawling. The guest's wife saved the situation, just in the nick of time. She kept the proper spirit of levity by biting Finch. Under these circumstances, his little joke fell flat. So did Finch. The guests finally departed, laughing and joking and bandaged at 12:30 A.M.

My gambit is simpler. When arriving at the Klavans', they find that I talk incessantly for perhaps the first twenty minutes. Then I fall asleep.

My conviction is that I must say what I have to say before I fall in a catatonic state and am lost to the assemblage forever. Unfortunately, I cannot fall asleep with finesse. I usually sit there, people say, with my eyes fully open, staring balefully into a crack in the living-room wall. People ask me questions, I am told, and I respond erratically. One may say, for instance, "What do you think of the situation in Laos?" I snap out a stock answer developed for such occasions: "Thirty-eight degrees and cloudy." Phyllis Klavan, a sensitive woman, can detect the precise point at which I am about to slip off into unconsciousness and, without a change of expression, slips by in her role of gracious hostess and drops hot coffee into my clenched fist. The results are not a pretty sight, but it is effective.

Naturally, these problems are classic and not confined to very early risers like ourselves. Undeniably, many of our readers are involved and as part of our attitude of public service, the following list of suggestions may help you to rid your home of unwanted guests at the proper hour, and leave you, night after night, serene and unfettered by annoyances, like the presence of old and trusted companions and the good feelings of true friendship:

(1) At nine-thirty, begin to yawn quietly. At first, smile self-consciously and say "Oops."

(2) At 9:50, stop saying "Oops."

(3) At 10:00, commence yawning noisily, especially if a woman is speaking. Pretend to stop the yawns unsuccessfully with your fist.

(4) At 10:15, remove your shoes and undo the first three buttons of your shirt. Scratch yourself on the chest heartily.

(5) At 10:30, hum softly *Auf Wiedersehen.* If it becomes obvious that the guests are not familiar with the tune, explain, like a disc jockey, that it is an old German song which means "So Long." If, by chance, you are not familiar with *Auf Wiedersehen* yourself, hum almost anything and explain that this is an old German song which means, "So Long." (This device works best if you do not hum *Stardust,* or *The Stars and Stripes Forever.*)

(6) At 11:00, leap to the sofa and scream boisterously, "Get out, damn it, haven't you got a home?" Then hum *Get the Hell Out,* which is an old German sentiment.

(7) At 6:15 A.M., look into the rear-view mirror, or the microphone, or whoever is before you, and say, "Thirty-eight clouds" or "Thirty cloud eights and degrees . . ."

CHAPTER 8

A Song of Songs

Music is, of course, an important part of radio's continuing appeal. At least it is a part of radio.

In any case, we play records. And despite what people say, the songs that get played on the air don't just get there by accident.

You are absolutely right. You *can* write better songs than those you hear today. We agree that it is amazing that the yowling, raucous, cacophonous drivel that is pressed onto some of those records finds its way to the public via the juke boxes and broadcasting media. You doubtless feel that you can write better music than that with one octave tied behind you.

So do we.

So does everybody we know.

The statistics that we usually invent suggest that there are approximately 150,000 songwriters in New York alone, give or take a few thousand. These people are not just talking about it, they are doing something about it. Mostly cursing.

Some of those thousands are actually fighting their way over the tangled paths which lead to eventual fortunes down the one primrose path that is Tin Pan Alley. Some finally do make it and revel in the glory and fame enjoyed by the Irving Berlins, the Cole Porters, Jimmy McHughs, and Milton Steiner.[1]

But one must be prepared to give up everything, live in a garret, eat short rations, forgo new clothing, abstain from drinking and smoking, and the Book-of-the-Month Club. To illustrate the difficulties indigenous to the road to fame, may we explore the hard fight put up by one of the quality songwriters of our time? She would tell you the story herself if you were able to discover her real name. But, until then, let us examine the career of Jackie Eisenhower, girl composer.

Jackie was a pleasant little girl who began writing songs at an early age. She was still in elementary school. While the other children were shouting "Ole ole ole in free!" and "Viva Castro!" Jackie was shouting flatted fifths and dominant chords. No one visited Jackie's little home without becoming part of an audience to one of Jackie's little tunes. At eight years of age, Jackie startled her mentors by announcing that the second stanza of *The Star-Spangled Banner* did not scan.

Her music teacher at Theodore Roosevelt High felt that Jackie might be better off out of the way, studying composition at some music college that was also out of the way. Her vocational counselor felt that Jackie might be better off becoming a gym teacher. Jackie's father felt that she

[1] Milton Steiner is the one who actually wrote the music of Berlin, Porter, and McHugh.

would be better off in some school where there were wealthy boys who did not expect too much out of marriage.

Jackie provided her parents with a series of neurotic scenes, complete with kicking and screaming and one threat to destroy herself by ingesting a 45 rpm record of Paul Anka's number-two hit. There was, consequently, no other course open to them but that of sending their highly strung, physically well-endowed child to the Juilliard School of Music to major in Bass Guitar and minor in Polynesian Health Chants. Off to New York went Jackie Eisenhower.

"Broadway, my Broadway!" Jackie murmured as she walked the famous street, the street of the famous. She refused to notice the dingy pictures of the dingy naked girls in the dingy shops. She was blind to the slot machines, the FOR RENT signs, the chewing gum sticking to her saddle shoes, the perpetually "going out of business" stores. She saw on Broadway only what she wanted to see—her name sputtering and sparkling overhead, right beside the Frozen Pizza marquee.

Her first year in New York was spent in pilgrimages, after school, to the mecca of popular music. Her ambition became more realistic: now she wanted only to hear her words and music on the lips of all America and to see all the coins of our land in her palm. "I hear America singing," she said defiantly, "but the bastards aren't singing my stuff." Knowing no one, having no entrée or connections, she was frustrated at every turn.

Eventually, through fellow students, Jackie was fortunate

enough to meet someone at a folk singing rally in Greenwich Village who informed her that to sell her material she must take it to a music *publisher*. Jubilant, Jackie and her friend returned to the rally to finish the last chorus of *John Henry*.

Although the music publishers are scattered throughout the Broadway area, it was to the largest covey that Jackie headed. When first she saw the Brill Building, in the trade known affectionately as the Brill B., she merely stood before it, legs akimbo and eyes aflutter. This is a ridiculous position to maintain but she was young. The directory of the building was speckled with the names of music publishers who had filled the ears of America since that prehistoric day when Guy Lombardo said to Lawrence Welk, "You call that music?" The names of the composers, lyricists, and arrangers who had entered those dirty golden doors would make a layman tingle; for song writers, the Brill Building is the Metropolitan Museum. Jackie stood there for a moment, ruminating about the talent, the inspiration, the royalties which had traversed those hallowed halls. Then she sought out a name which caught her imagination and headed for the publisher's office. Surely the racy epithets scrawled on the walls of the elevator should have discouraged a less determined person, but Jackie had waited too long and had gone too far. She thought that Wholesome Music Inc. would be a chromium-plated, silverlined, jewel-encrusted haven. What she found when she entered the office was that it was heavily cobwebbed, obsolescent, and apparently insolvent. Jackie was about to back out of the office, disillusionment fairly etched on her pretty face.

"What is it, darling?" a man shouted from behind a mountainous pile of dusty records and manuscripts. It was Mr. Wholesome himself, a man in his rough fifties, and definitely not a man who had seen many real people of late.

"I've made a mistake, I'm afraid," gasped Jackie.

"Just a second, bubby," Mr. Wholesome replied, enthralled with the delightful honey-colored hair, the youthful glow of her skin, the unyielding shape of this nineteen-year-old beauty. He saw talent peeping through.

"I've got a few manuscripts . . ." Jackie said cautiously.

"Manuscripts?"

"Yes, my music . . ."

"Who reads music?" Mr. Wholesome said. "Maybe you could better play one of them études for me."

Jackie shoved away the accumulated dust from the top of a piano bench, using her manila envelope as a plow. She took off her gloves, her hat, her coat, and sat down on the bench to begin the first number.

"My music is different from the junk you hear nowadays," she said brightly.

"Of course, darling," said Mr. Wholesome, standing behind her with his vast stomach resting in the small of her back. In an attempt to provide encouragement, he placed his hands on her shoulders.

"Shall I sing it while I play?" she asked demurely.

"Sing, baby, sing," Mr. Wholesome intoned, kneading her upper arms. Jackie began in her clear, sweet soprano to sing the lyrics of *My Heart Is a Bower of Roses*. She sang her heart out with her words "Although my head opposes/ My heart is a bower of roses/ I give, and that presupposes/ It's love.[2] As she sang, the pure simplicity of the melody moved the publisher to the point that he could not restrain himself from unbuttoning the top buttons of her blouse and kissing the back of her young neck.

"You're making my pitch rise!" Jackie interjected without turning around.

"Yours too?" Mr. Wholesome asked delightedly. Having finished the song with an entrancing arpeggio, Jackie pushed Wholesome's hands from her ribs. She turned to face the music publisher. His brow, she noticed, was damp with perspiration. He was excited about her music!

"You like it?" she asked proudly.

"It's got me all hot and bothered," he answered, running the back of his hand over his brow.

"Then you'll accept it?" she asked triumphantly.

Wholesome stepped backward so quickly he almost stumbled over the grimy cuspidor. Where was this child's respect, he wondered. Didn't this novice realize that she was dealing with the company that had almost published *I'll Never Say Smile Again,* a song almost recorded by Frank Sinatra.

"Just a minute, darling, not so hasty."

"What's the matter?"

"Well, it needs work. It needs help from a song doctor. Phil will have to knock a few rough edges off here and there."

[2] Copyright 1963, Wholesome Music, Inc.

"Phil?"

"Phil's one of the best. I wouldn't take it without Phil should give it a hand." His tone was one of finality.

"Phil, the song doctor, won't destroy my message, will he? I mean, my song is different from the junk you hear nowadays," Jackie said cautiously.

"That's one of your troubles, baby," Wholesome informed her. "So Phil will take a small percentage, but that's all. It'll still basically be your song." Taking this thought under consideration, Jackie picked up her manila envelope and began to extract another song.

"Would you like to see everything I've got?" she asked.

"Before we're through, I'll see, I'll see," Mr. Wholesome answered softly as though singing *September Song*. Jackie put her coat and gloves on, shook hands and left in a cloud of enthusiasm. Wholesome saw her to the door, muttering after Jackie left, "She shakes hands."

When she finally heard from Phil, it was an invitation to visit his apartment. Jackie refused. Phil invited himself to her apartment; she refused. So Phil, maintaining he could only work in apartments, did not meet Jackie in person until their meeting at a small recording studio. The recording studio was one of hundreds which tic-tac-toe across the face of the theater district. They are used primarily for the recording of demos, of demonstration records. A "demo," it had best be explained, is a record of a song made to show to executives of recording companies who cannot read music either.

When Phil saw Jackie approaching him in the studio, he saw a girl of nineteen, flush with the nubile magnificence of beautiful youth. She was pretty too. Past the pimply stage, Phil thought. She was sheer spectacle for the pimply thirty-year-old music doctor.

"So *you're* the chick, eh sweetie baby?" Phil said courteously.

"I am Jackie Eisenhower," Jackie said with womanly grace.

"Any relation to the other Eisenhower?" Phil asked cautiously.

"Who?" Jackie replied ingenuously.

"Never mind, pussycat, I heard about you from the Brill B. I got eyes for you."

"Have you helped my song, Phil? It's different from the junk you hear nowadays, you know," she said hopefully. She had to use his first name because it was the accepted method of address in the music business. Besides, no one had ever told her his last name.

"I straightened that out, Tiger. When we cut it, you'll flip. Now, we got to cut the demo. I already had a singer and a piano man fall by. We got to play it cagey. We cut this disc simple, so the record company we show it to don't think we're telling them how to cut it. But at the same time we stick in a gimmik so if they don't dig *bower,* they dig the gimmik."

"But my music is different from the junk you hear nowa—"

"I *dig,* lover-girl, but that's what you got Philsie for. I straighten out all that jazz. It rocks. It rocks." He laughed with pleasure, then he called in the singer and the pianist. He shouted to the engineer to ready himself for the "take," the girl pianist ran through the music, and the vocalist took one look at Jackie and ran through his date book.

"Here's for luck, wild one," Phil said, and he grabbed Jackie and kissed her passionately, simultaneously running his hands under her sweater. Before she had time to beat her fists on his chest, he had retreated to the control room and was barking unintelligible orders over the intercom system into the studio.

The vocalist spit his gum into a corner, the pianist hit a chord and an ON AIR light denoted that the recording was in progress.

"Pydee bow bing!" the vocalist began. "Pydee bow bing!" He snapped his fingers to the rhythm as he continued into the lyrics.

"Wait a minute!" Jackie screamed.

"Cut!" yelled the engineer.

"What the hell?" Phil snapped into the intercom.

"What is this 'pydee bow bing'?" Jackie asked tearfully.

"Pussycat, I *told* you, I straightened it out for you." Phil crooned into the intercom.

"Hurry up, pussycat," said the vocalist, "I got three more of these things to do before lunch."

"I got a session with Perry and Julie," said the girl pianist, biting her nails.

"But the song, my sweet little song, it'll sound like all the other junk you hear nowadays," Jackie said with large, classic tears in her clear eyes.

"Don't be a pioneer, Scubadoll," Phil soothed her through the magic of the talk-back system. "Take two," he thundered. The artists resumed their rendition, sang it

through and were dismissed. The vocalist retrieved his
gum, grabbed Jackie and kissed her. The pianist gathered
the music, handed it to Jackie and kissed her. Phil returned to the studio carrying a black metal record. "Pay
them off, Lovebunny," he told the composer. Jackie found
that she owed the pianist $15 and the vocalist $10. She
had to pay the recording studio $12.50 and in doing so
realized that she had exhausted her money from home for
the week.

"OK, Chickie, we hit the A and R man, cha cha cha,"
Phil said as he gathered up Jackie and her effects and
headed out of the building.

Then Phil stunned Jackie with his news: she was going
to meet Lance Vinyl, the A and R man (Artists and Rep-
ertoire head) of Gelt records. When you think of RCA,
Columbia, Capitol, you think of Gelt, even if you don't
think too highly of any of them.

Vinyl, as any *aficionado* of the popular musical arts is
aware, is sort of a musical Leonard Bernstein. He has his
own radio program of interviews and songs and his re-
nowned television program Lyrics with Lance. He is a con-
ductor, flautest, and a spokesman for the music business.
His was the quote which has been cited in *The Wall Street
Journal* as the credo of the music business. At a Harvard
Business School symposium, he had said, "The aim of the
American music industry is to uplift the nation's intrinsi-
cally excellent musical tastes. On the other hand, if the
public wants crap, we'll give it to them."

With all deference to his intellectualism, Lance Vinyl
turned out to be unforbidding to Jackie, at least in his ap-

pearance. His graying hair and his British muttonchop mustache set off his sartorial device of clothing himself from head to toe in cashmere. There he is, Jackie thought, a mature man in cashmere suit, shirt, tie, belt, and sox. Only his shoes deviated from the pattern, they were obviously of purest suède. He spoke in subdued tones, modulating his voice so that it had a slight drone which rose at the end of each sentence.

"Jackie, honey, how good to see you," Vinyl said, looking Jackie straight in the bosom. Phil, having introduced the two, saw that his presence was no longer demanded.

"Well, splitsville, man," Phil cheerfully said, "I'll leave you two kids alone." Phil backed out of the office.

The office was a model jungle. It was furnished with zebra-striped chairs and tables. The wall behind the desk bore a shield and crossed spears from a highly regarded African tribe. Next to the window was a beautifully mounted Agapa head surrounded by wax masapanthas blooms. A mammoth couch the size of a double bed, with elephant tusks at either end was the only uncluttered piece of furniture in the room.

"Now, little Jackie," Lance said, motioning her to sit beside him on the couch, "what's this all about?"

"Well, sir, I have a demo here and I thought if you liked it we could have a hit song," Jackie said breathlessly striving for the hard sell.

But Lance Vinyl had a sell of his own. "Why don't we just hop over to my place and put it on the hi-fi where we can hear it in comfort? The place has a self-service elevator and a forgetful doorman."

"Well, couldn't we just hear my song here? I'd like to hear it again to tell the truth. And besides, I'd better get back to Juilliard; just to get here I had to cut Cymbals and Drums Phase II."

Lance pulled Jackie down next to him on the couch. "Bunnyrabbit, let's just stay here and make beautiful music then," he said with a flat laugh, his mustache twitching ever so slightly.

"Please, Mr. Vinyl, I think I have heard *that* song before," Jackie pleaded, drawing away.

"Baby, I only have to hear half of your song, you know. Phil owns the other half." He was nibbling on her ear.

So great was her astonishment at hearing how her property had diminished, Jackie could not even protest. In addition, with his mustache tickling her earlobe, she was so close to a record she could almost hear it.

"All right, how many records do you think it will sell?" she asked angrily.

"Millions," Lance said, kissing her neck.

"But you haven't heard it yet," she said, trying to fend him off.

"Ummmmmmm, I hear beautiful music already." With this remark, from the excited A and R man, Jackie stood up. She took the record off the desk and placed it on the turntable. She turned the amplifier up loud. Lance looked at her as the first pydee bow bing came issuing forth. Lance licked his lips slowly.

"I mean now, really," Jackie said in a quasi-business-like tone, "what do you think?"

"You'll have to stand the recording costs, out of your

royalties-in-advance," he said, matter-of-factly, sitting up.

"Oh, I can get $12.50 easily enough," she said with exuberance.

"Twelve hundred and fifty dollars for one of our sessions," Lance said cheerfully. "Then you only got *half* a song."

"How long will it take to make money?" There was terror in her lovely clear eyes.

"With the royalty deal we give, you gotta sell maybe a couple million." His voice was cold now.

"Isn't it a big country, I mean, Lance?" she asked in a small voice.

"Not *that* big, baby," he answered. Lance was filing his nails now as he stood by his desk.

"You really think we could make beautiful music together, Lance?" he heard Jackie say in a quietly resigned manner.

"I can hear the opening notes now," he answered blowing at his fingertips. He looked up and saw that Jackie had moved back to the couch.

"What songs do you know, Lance?" she was asking.

4

CHAPTER 9

Home Is Like No Place

On Long Island, about twenty-two miles from the radio station, there are two houses. They are only three miles from each other, but the people within live in two different worlds. Finch lives in a quietly modern house, furnished in contemporary décor, with a few antiques here and there for contrast. I live in a noisily traditional house, a Cape Cod, furnished in Old American décor, with a few decent pieces of furniture here and there. It is rather simple, in a household which caters to four boys and their friends, to convert modern to antique.

Both Mrs. Klavan and Mrs. Finch were schoolteachers in their halcyon days, but they were forced to give it up when progressive education all but eliminated the teaching of halcyons. Their experience stands them in good stead. The two Finch children, in my opinion, are a joy to behold. Kindly, bright, courteous, and mature, twelve-year-old Greg and nine-year-old Virginia are perhaps the nicest children I have ever seen. It is, to be sure, quite impossible for the Finches to have raised such delightful children themselves; obviously the credit must be given to an occasional sneak visit by a grandparent.

The Klavan children, on the other hand (their usual position), range in age from thirteen-year-old Ross, through nine-year-old Drew and down to the six-year-old twins, Scott and Laurence. They are unmanageable, discourteous, and on the average not so brilliant as their father. Finch, the soul of compatibility, disagrees with my appraisal. He feels that I am not severe enough. This may be because, according to him, visitors to our house are as likely to be attacked by wild children as they are by a wild dog. Dog? Yes, we have one, large and active. He began normally enough, as a sort of puppy, but he retrogressed. The veterinarian maintains that this is because of his environment, and is in an effort to hold his own. In any case, we find him a comfort.

Our at home personalities are quite different, too. Finch is a shouter. He is a man quite capable of raising his bellowing voice until the mirror on the medicine cabinet cracks. I, on the other hand, am chicken. Afraid and shy of the world, I'm dead certain that if I yell, one of the children, or my wife, will destroy me. Finch is a screamer, I am a seether. When Finch is mad, he will tell anybody off and in no uncertain terms. I try to imply with funny little lines that I object to something. If implication does not work, my technique changes: I hide in a closet and sulk for days. Inasmuch as Mrs. Klavan never throws anything out, it is often difficult to find a comfortable place to sulk.

People ask if we are clowns at home. The truth is that we are both worriers. We are, in fact, worriers on the job as well. If there is nothing to worry about, we create things. It is a splendid day when we can convince those around us that we are losing the cold war, that the air is polluted, and that sex is fattening.

Because of these tendencies, and demanding jobs, we have to have our forms of recreation. Finch has gone through a plethora of hobbies. And going through a plethora is even more difficult than going through the Holland Tunnel. For a time, he was a ham radio operator. This seemed appropriate; he was a ham radio performer as well and they seemed to me to blend nicely. More recently, he has allowed his amateur radio work to slip away. In his words, "There are enough amateurs operating commercial radio stations." He decided to sell out and turned a quick profit selling his equipment to Mitchell Katz, one of the engineers who do our show. It was months later before he found that Mitchell Katz had made a tremendous profit by selling the equipment to the radio station itself. I cannot bring myself to tell him yet that the station, which had sold the equipment to Finch in the first place, made a tremendous profit by losing it and claiming the insurance.

Both Betty and Dee Finch have tried their hand at flying small planes. Both received their private pilot licenses, but as with a friend who is getting too rich and dangerous to keep up with, they decided to drop flying before it dropped them.

After ham radio, and flying, came a boat. Finch owned a beautiful boat for one season. Then a hurricane at Montauk Point destroyed it. Finch was relieved; it saved him the expense of having it hauled out of the water and stored for the winter. Encouraged, I tried my hand at owning a boat. Because of an innate sense of thrift, I bought a boat in partnership with a neighbor. Actually then, to be honest, I owned only half a boat. My half boat was not destroyed in a hurricane, but my digestion was. I had expected to be seasick, and I was, but an unforeseen difficulty was that each time I got off the boat, I was landsick. I sold out. But the other owner and I decided it was better to have loved the sea and lost my meals than never to have launched at all.

Now, I have become a nut on photography. Our home includes a complete photographic darkroom. This was already installed when we bought the house and Phyllis insists that we bought the house for the darkroom. That is silly and I cannot agree, but it is true that the house was advertised as a Cape Cod with two bathrooms and an enlarger.

One of the Klavan classic efforts is a sound movie, based on the story of the Alamo, and using my children and their friends as actors. Unfortunately, the picture, filmed over a period of time, was never finished because in each scene the stars got taller and their voices got deeper. Somehow, this seems to destroy the credibility of the Alamo story.

Appropriately for two men whose stories are being told in this form, both Finch and I are insatiable readers. Finch is addicted to works of non-fiction. He reads relatively little fiction. The last novel he recalls reading was *Tarzan and His Flying Machine,* by Edgar Rice Burroughs. Finch rec-

ognized immediately that the thesis of the story was pre-
posterous and that neither Tarzan nor Edgar Burroughs
would ever get the thing off the ground. Somehow, this destroyed the credibility of fiction for him and he has turned
instead to a wide ranging diet of books on general non-
fiction subjects. He also cares little for movies. He claims
that the last motion picture he saw was Army Training
Film TF 247 A, *Personal Hygiene and Health Habits*. He
cried over that one.

On the other hand, I read novels. After all, my business
is humor and you never can tell when you're going to be
able to wring a really hearty chuckle out of *Lady Chat-
terley's Lover* or *The Carpetbaggers*.

Thank you for letting us let you come into our living
rooms, but I hasten to close the subject because, after all,
two performers cannot get caught too long in a condition
where they seem to be like everyone else. There is star
quality to consider. A man either has it or he doesn't. And
when he has it, it is a precious, indefinable quantity that
causes him to live in fear. Someday it may slip away, quite
beyond his control.

I never expect to have the problem.

Every star gives off an aura. He is above the cut of normality. They have an almost chemical phosphorescence
about them and this at times has very little to do with talent. Some people are stars and others are not. Just as some
people are beautiful or tall or Greek Orthodox. But a real
star is evident from the moment you see him across a
crowded room. Somehow you know, even then.

The only reason to discuss star quality in a book of this sort is if there is something of value in it for the reader. Not every reader can be a star. But any reader who has had the experience we have, of watching and observing the stars in action, over the years, learns that there are imitable as well as inimitable characteristics.

If one is born a star, one never has to ask himself how to behave. It comes naturally. But by observing behavior, we can acquire those elusive star symptoms. For example, after the eighth or ninth martini, a star does not fall down drunk, as an ordinary person would. He begins to decline, makes a deathless statement, beautifully couched and epigrammatic—"The world is a big fat bastard!"—and then swoons spectacularly to the floor. He may shout to the bartender before he expires: "I've been poisoned." *Never,* under any circumstances, does he allow himself to take on that commonplace green tinge and moan softly, "I'm going to be sick." A star is never sick. Dead, yes. Ill, of course. But sick—never.

To be a star, you must first of all never do or say the expected thing. If people expect you to agree, disagree. If they expect you to disagree, agree, even if it hurts. After an interval, they will come to expect you to do the unexpected. Then reverse your field and do what everybody else would do. This process takes considerable time and effort, but it has its rewards. Your family must cooperate. Unless they are aware that you are becoming a star, they will fail to adopt a tolerant attitude and they too must prepare themselves for your new way of life. Begin by one evening, shortly after supper, throwing a tantrum. Fall to the rug and scream, "It's more than a sensitive person like myself can bear!" If you are a teenager and your parents would like to know what it is that is too much to bear, answer "Everything!" If a frightened member of the family urges you to see a doctor, announce that the doctor is a "pseudo intellectual mumbler of half-baked psychological mumbo-jumbo."

Be flamboyant in your opinions. If someone should ask, "What do you think of the President of the United States?" lash back with a forceful, "Hah!" Then, add slowly and with a sneer, "I'd just as soon see Genghis Khan in the White House." Recovering, your antagonist may say, "Oh, then, you're a——" (mentioning the name of the opposition leader) "man?" At this point, you can shine. Look at your questioner in pity and then say, "That idiot. That poor, misled idiot." If the questioner pushes for clarification, look away and mutter grandly, "Dammit, I don't want to talk about it any more."

Never answer the telephone. A star does not answer the telephone. When he is called to the phone, he acknowledges the call with a flippancy ("Castro, here.") Or if the call is obviously serious business, he jokes. ("What are you calling me at this hour for? So it's a contract? I don't care if they want to fly me to the moon, I think Bermuda is a bore and I wouldn't go back to the Mediterranean again on a bet.") This dialogue is particularly useful for establishing your continued presence in the area and permits you to keep your job in the mail room.

A star always offers his or her advice on anything, preferably when not asked. Remember, when you say something, it means something, it isn't just anybody talking. Always preface your remarks with a modest disclaimer: "Naturally, my opinion doesn't mean much, but . . ." or "Of course, this is none of my business . . ." or, a touch of refinement, "Look, I know you're too worldly to be offended at this, and I want you to stop me if you like, but . . ." This technique is a wonderful ego builder for you and, unless you add words after the "but" it does nicely by your companion. If you decide to go on with the sentence, the effect changes. For example, you might choose to join a conversation, saying, "Look, nobody asked me, and perhaps I'm imposing, but what is a girl with a face like yours doing with that hairdo?"

When anyone asks if you have heard a particular joke, nod affirmatively. It does not do for a star to be in a position where ordinary people can surpass him, even in telling jokes. But if someone begins telling a joke before you have had a chance to declare that you have already heard it, allow him to begin, and then say without smiling, "I hate jokes!" and walk away. If a dinner guest has a particularly witty one-liner, say unhappily, "You dirty rat." When he expresses wonderment at the outburst, answer, "You didn't think that was funny when I said it." If you have never seen the offender before, an alternative retort is possible: "I think that is in exquisitely poor taste. But then *you* couldn't possibly know that."

Finally, as a star, you will find yourself consulted by young people anxious to advance themselves in their careers. Meekly, they will consult you for bits and pieces of information. Naturally, you cannot answer them. For one thing, a star doesn't know why he or she is as good as he or she is. After all, it is only the commonplace talents that can be articulated. The best advice for the young hopeful is, "Kid, get out of the business."

But, quite without meaning it, I find that the narrative has moved here away from the placid serenities of home life and back into the irresistible attractions of show business. Time, then, for another look at the real world.

CHAPTER 10

Victor Verse of the People

Among the motley crew of imaginary characters who punctuate the morning hours of our program, none is more revered, by us, than Victor Verse, our poet lariat. He is to us what Robert Frost was to Washington, Carl Sandburg to Chicago, maybe more. He developed one day when Finch said, in the middle of a commercial that was expiring from lack of enthusiasm, "Be a poet." In such an illegitimate fashion was Victor Verse born. Our story about him is that he is actually a man who is unrecognized, but an artist nonetheless, an artist who wrote poetry on soda fountain mirrors with Redi-Whip. Apparently he was not too successful because as he was writing "Life is tedious, uninspired—" his boss approached and finished it with "Grab your coat and hat, you're fired." Victor has commented on most of life's vagaries, often expressing in little verses what we do not have enough guts to express in editorials.

We have decided to include here some of the more cogent poetry from his forthcoming volume of poetry; his first threecoming were also rejected. The book, to be entitled, *Some of My Really Great Ones* will be just full of highly expressive verse. It is with great difficulty that we were able to select the few inclusions. It was difficult because the Redi-Whip kept running down the pages.

(The publication of these verses for profit or gain is strictly forbidden by the commissioner of baseball and is subject to prosecution. All rights are reserved and all reserves can be activated in case of emergency.)

THE SECRET, OURS

Our second place in the race for space/may cause us, some
    say, to lose face.
But the fault lies not with our guys,
Who are spies.
But with their guys,
Who are wise.
We check our people every day with the FBI and the CIA.
And they all wear a badge or a shield or pin
To keep from leaking out what's "in."
There's no flow of photo info to direct
Or show where connectors couple or couplers connect.
No maps or blueprints or pix to say
How what goes up must come down or stay.
Our security is inured with surety.
It's directed, protected, inspected; dissected if suspected
Of impurity.
So when we have something new after all that fuss.
You can be sure our secret's safe with us.
Of course,

A general may hint to LOOK.

A scientist may write a book.

A senator on TV may say that they'll never beat the good
old USA because of something new that's on the way.

And the newspapers intimate.

And magazines insinuate.

And toymakers speculate and build models that approxi-
mate.

And the toy with the envoy from the iron curtain is on the
way home and *he's* fairly certain.

So everyone wonders how they have figured out how to
bring our thing down to earth over there.

While over here it's still up in the air.

INJUSTICE

There's nothing so terribly cruel or unfair
As a nearsighted man in a barber chair.
To others, clean shaven, he wasn't bad, was he?
But the nearsighted man will always look fuzzy.

THE DESTRUCTION OF THE IAMBIC PENTAMETER
an historic recitation

Who let Alaska and Hawaii in
To join our sacred union?
Who let Alaskans and Hawaiians

Enlarge the old communion?
When we had only forty-eight
For poets, what proclitivity
To rhyme the eight with state and great
But what will rhyme with fivity?

EMOTION
I hate
Weight.

ART

To hell with Norman Rockwell
And the insurance company ads.
Their pretty pictures mock well the true-to-life plight of
dads.
Remember the one where Daddy comes home after a
hard day of endurance,
His appearance of perseverance and adherence in strain-
ing, and braining in sustaining the family?
And his youngster skates up to him, throws those little
arms around him and says, "Hya Daddy!"
Well?
Insurance companies, lumber mills, saving banks, chemical

firms, Saturday Evening Post and the National Geo-
graphic and Norman Rockwell.

Go to hell.

You know what kids say?

"Whatja bring me?"

"I told him hello already, Ma."

"Pop, you're standing on third."

Or

Not a word.

That's what kids say after a persevering, adhering, day of
endurance.

You purveyors of magazines and insurance.

Occasionally, Dad will be blessed with conversation like
can we go to the movies, can I have baseball cards of
all the kids in school today I was the worst, or she
hit me first.

That's what.

Where was Norman Rockwell when
the poor dog was painted and perfume scented
the toothpaste tainted and the car door dented
the doll in the oven was near cremation
and the cellar threatened with irrigation
the best bush with BB's fully leaded
and the kids all hiding cause they knew they'd get it?

Norman, about your work—I don't mean to detract

You think you're realistic.

To me, you're abstract.

CHAPTER 11

A Nice Place to Visit

In later chapters, it will be shown that Klavan and Finch are true internationalists (Chapter 15, 'On the Double Talk,' illuminates our experience on the steppes of Rome, for example). At the risk of seeming empirical (Latin for Empire State) we are world citizens, both having been forced to leave the country at one time or another. Having been to Europe and funny little places like that, we find that we are eminently qualified to compare our own country with other nations. Because our President has been making attempts recently to encourage tourism in the United States, we have decided that it is time for us to speak out in behalf of this country. We would like foreigners to visit the United States and to discover that in spite of the vast sums that we dole out for foreign aid, we are not all bad.

The problems that future visitors to our shores will have when they reach New York are manifold. We are, therefore, compiling a guide book for those lucky folks who reach the land of liberty but are unfamiliar with its habits and customs. We are also including a glossary of words and phrases destined to assist any visitor around New York City. If you know anyone from a foreign land who might be interested, tear out these pages and send them along to him.

ANSWERS TO FOREIGNERS' QUESTIONS
ABOUT THE UNITED STATES

(1) Can I drink the water? *Ans:* Although most Americans believe that water is only a mixer, it is perfectly safe to drink the water.

(2) What are foods that are safe to eat? *Ans:* Most foods are frozen or canned and are not prepared by home-makers, therefore, are safe. In restaurants, however, typical American foods are: spaghetti, shishkebob, chow mein, filet mignon, wiener schnitzel, borscht, and pastrami.

(3) How are hotel accommodations? *Ans:* Expensive.

(4) How will I find taxi service? *Ans:* Expensive, unless it rains. Then you will not find it at all.

(5) How are American girls? *Ans:* Expensive.

(6) What kind of clothing should I bring with me? *Ans:* It is unimportant, most American women haven't a thing to wear.

(7) What are some cultural things to see? *Ans:* Museums, libraries, theaters, and television game shows.

(8) Where can I find members of the opposite sex to fraternize with? *Ans:* See answer to question 7.

(9) What is the most important thing to keep in mind in New York? *Ans:* The same thing that is always on your mind.

(10) In case of emergency what should I do? *Ans:* Join the John Birch society.

LANGUAGE GLOSSARY

In order to make your pronunciation difficulties less pronounced, we are including a phonetic guide with a translation for our foreign guests.

(*Arriving at customs*)
Lem mesee wha chagot heah.
(May I see your baggage, please.)

Gotcha papehs?
(May I see your passport and immunization certificate?)

Cum on hoo yoo kid in?
(Have you anything to declare?)

Wear da hellsa hack?
(Can you tell me where I can find a taxi, please?)

(SIGNS, *as written in the American language and translated into English*)

YIELD TO THE RIGHT
(Refrain from political argument)

SPEED LIMIT 55 MILES
(Speed limit 65 miles)

RADAR SPEED ZONE
(Uncontrolled and unpatrolled)

KEEP OFF THE GRASS
(Picnic area)

MOVING STAIRS
(No more for you!)

GREATEST EPIC EVER TO BE FILMED . . . SEXA-
TIONAL . . . SHOCKING . . .
(A movie.)

RESTAURANT GLOSSARY

Weer fool up.
(For two dollars, you may have the best seat in the
house.)
Wha' joo rekamend, weight-ah?
(Goodbye, cruel world.)
Wee have *verry* nize rib sov beeef.
(Watch out for the ribs of beef.)
R yoo' memburrs ov da die nurs klob?
(This is one I'm putting over on Uncle Sam as a
business deduction.)
Mi kompleemints two da shef!
(Murderer!)

MEETING PEOPLE

Hy yah.
(How do you do, it is a great honor and pleasure to
meet you.)
Whadya no?
(Have you read any good books, seen any good mov-
ies, done anything interesting, how is your family and
is everything all right at the office?)
Wheel havta get two getter onea dese daze.
(This is goodbye, you'll never hear from me again.)
You bleeve in luv at furst site?
(I have immoral intentions toward you.)

Ima nonkon formist.

(I'm a married man, but don't let that bother you, sweetie.)

I reel-y shunt be doing this.

(I'm a married woman, but don't let that bother you, sweetie.)

Ah hah', ye-ah.

(Yes.)

Uh hu, naah.

(No.)

OBSOLETE WORDS, NO LONGER USED IN THE UNITED STATES:

Please

Thank you

Pardon me

You're welcome

We certainly hope that your stay in the United States will be a pleasant one and that you will carry back to your native land the fervent wishes of all Americans. See yah.

CHAPTER 12

Ask a Stupid Question

The changing tide of broadcasting has not washed out one of the most reliable time-fillers ever known, the celebrity interview. Klavan and Finch conduct no actual interviews although we have many of an imaginary and fraudulent nature. Some of our more erudite experts are: Dr. Kology, our analyst; Victor Verse, the poet lariat of the program; Col. Korn, our Kansas City television station manager; Fred Freelance, the outstanding radio/TV performer in the country; and Paul Paul Jr., scion of a wealthy Philadelphia family who is so egocentric he suffers from sibling rivalry although he is an only child.

The main reason for eliminating real interviews was that, with two interviewers, they tended to get unwieldy. It is also just as true that instead of real interviews we can better use the time for real commercials. In a day and age when our system is threatened from all sides, we don't want to feel that we are throttling free enterprise.

There are really only two kinds of interviews, the standard interview and a newer approach, the psychological or depth interview. The standard interview is so standard, indeed, that most sound exactly alike. You hear almost the identical questions and answers as the celebrity passes from show to show, plugging his latest movie, book, or record. At times it seems that only the interviewer is changed to protect the identity of the station.

We would like to make it possible for our friends to run through a celebrity interview with the person of your choice in your own home at any time you desire. All you have to do is (1) leave the radio off, (2) consult your paper for details of who is in town, (3) and fill in the blanks in the interview provided. Neatness does not count and originality may disqualify you:

INTERVIEWER: And now, ladies and gentlemen, it's time to present (*use full name*). Thank you so much for coming to talk to our radio friends, (*first name only*).

GUEST: Thank *you* so much for having me here, you know whenever I'm in New York, I can't wait to be on your show.

INTERVIEWER: Tell us, ———, what brings you to town?

GUEST: Well, you know me and New York—a regular love affair. I can't stay away too long, I get homesick. I was sitting on one of those tiny beaches on the Riviera and I said, "I've got to get back to New York—" and here I am!

INTERVIEWER: Well—

GUEST: Besides, my new ——— is out and (*chuckle*) I just wanted to get around and see how it's doing.

INTERVIEWER: How—

GUEST: Oh, it's just thrilling! Just marvelous to see the

reception it got. You know, there are people who said that my new ———— is just too advanced for the American public. But I said, "Well now, that's just wrong to underestimate the taste and knowledge of the American people. And especially the people in this, the greatest, largest town on earth!" Don't you think so?

INTERVIEWER: Of cour—

GUEST: Our new ———— put out by ———— in cooperation with ———— is just $—— and although that's a little higher than usual, I hope your audience will think it's more than worth it.

INTERVIEWER: Well, I haven't had a chance to—

GUEST: Oh, I'll make a note of that and put you down on the list.

INTERVIEWER: Thanks, now would you like to tell us a little bit about it?

GUEST: Well, I don't want to, you know, destroy anyone's curiosity, but it's an interpretation—no you better make that a reinterpretation—of the very thing we all hold dear. Everybody, just everybody will love it, it's just $—— and I hope that there's a long waiting list. Did I mention the name?

INTERVIEWER: Yes. I'm glad to hear about it. I think it's something that was crying to be done.

GUEST: We like to think so.

INTERVIEWER: What are your plans after this?

GUEST: Well, I'm going to have to take a little rest at Lake Tahoe after this and then it's, ha ha, back to the drawing board.

INTERVIEWER: Another ———?

GUEST: Yes. We're going to do a sequel to this one because we think it's going to answer a need. We feel that it was something that was crying to be done.

INTERVIEWER: I think so. Tell the audience, ———, where did you get your start?

GUEST: Oh! Oh that, well, I began in Cleveland, but when I saw the way things went in this business, I said to myself, "You've got to go to Hollywood or New York." You know, right before I came into town, I was getting ready for this trip, I realized how little the American people know about ———. So, I decided to tour and tell them a little about it, especially in the (*north, south, east, or west*). The price of my ——— is $——— and it may be a little high. But it was crying to be done. It may be a little high.

INTERVIEWER: I think so. No, I mean it *was* crying to be done. Well, thank you so much for coming here today and chatting with us, ———.

GUEST: Thank you for having me on your wonderful show. It's a pleasure.

INTERVIEWER: Thank you, come back again when you're in New York.

GUEST: Thank *you*, it's always a pleasure to be on your show when I'm in New York.

INTERVIEWER: Thank you.

GUEST: Thank *you*.

Such conventional conversations are, more and more, missing from the broadcast scene these days. Today, on television particularly, there is a tendency to approach the interview on a plane that is frankly psychological. To give you an example, we have transcribed a typical interview from the television show "Here's Bigtime U.S.A.," which is seen daily on one of the more popular channels:

ANNOUNCER: Bigtime USA—with your "star" reporter, Ella Bindle. Today's guest is Rick T. Ford, actor, painter, bon vivante and star of Global-International's new feature in Technicolor and multapluravision, now being featured at your Loew's theater, *Son of a Beast.* Here's Ella.

ELLA: Now Rick darling, I notice as I peruse through your lovely Beverly Hills home here that you have accumulated a gorgeous collection of paintings and sculptures.

RICK: Actually, Ella, I painted those pictures myself. I—

ELLA: Painted them yourself? How versatile!

RICK: And those art objects are just some old things I knocked out of granite while I was down at the Pasadena Playhouse waiting for the big break.

ELLA: How manually dextrous! How about those quaint little footstools?

RICK: Well, I built those after I finished the fireplace.

ELLA: And that patio and that screened-in porch?

RICK: Oh, I knocked those out while I was waiting for the cement in the swimming pool to set.

ELLA: Rick! Rick! What is this need to prove yourself?

RICK: Wha?

ELLA: This hypersensitive drive to build with your hands.

You seem obsessed with the need to create solid things, whole objects.

RICK: I, eh—I—

ELLA: Can't you see it? Can't you see that this is a manifestation of some inner urge that says to those of us who just observe, "See, see me with the dirt on my hands. I'm not just a gorgeous-looking, wealthy movie actor, I'm a full man."

RICK: I didn't really think of that. I know when I was a little boy back in Cleveland, my mother used to send me out to—

ELLA: Mother had a large influence on you?

RICK: Well, not exactly, see I had this mother and this father and—

ELLA: In your recent picture, "16.2," you played a sensitive, almost lost young man, searching, seeking some sign of affirmation. Was there torture in you when you played that role? What were you thinking?

RICK: Would you like to see some ashtrays and bookends I made last weekend? I painted Indian dancers on the—

ELLA: Rick, does an actor like yourself *lose* himself in his roles?

RICK: Do you like beaded leather belts?

ELLA: I mean, does someone like you, with a problem, become another person? Or is an actor like yourself, with a problem, able to transpire above character, establish an ambivalence and yet remain yourself? Are you fully aware of the subconscious new you that was written for you to interpret?

RICK: Problem?

ELLA: Yes, it must be obvious to you as it is to your many beloved fans that in the role of Rorie, in the *Misfits of the West*, you were the weakling—killing to prove your masculinity that you doubted so strongly. Was this a traumatic experience, inserting yourself in the role or did you feel at home?

RICK: Problem?

ELLA: Oh friends of television land, look around you. See what this capable young actor has made for himself. A castle of manliness. A bulwark of masculinity. A fortress against femininity. Isn't it obvious to you, Rick, that you are leaning on all this to reassure yourself?

RICK: Reassure myself? Would you like to see the plumbing I installed in—

ELLA: What about Sharon Rourschak and you? Is that all talk?

RICK: We're just good friends.

ELLA: Your tacit evasion gives us a clue, Rick. There really is no girl in your life, is there?

RICK: There is no particular girl but I have many friends. I have dates.

ELLA: *Name one!*

RICK: Listen, Bindle, this is unfair, to strip bare my private life. I mean, I'm sure your viewers don't want to be bored with my petty doings.

ELLA: Oh, Rick, doesn't it become obvious at last. Can't you see it? Have you sublimated it so far? Can't you see what it is that has happened?

RICK: What? What?

ELLA: Your p-r-o-b-l-e-m?

RICK: *I don't have any problem!* Now, let's go down this hall a little further. I'm sure your viewers would like to see some of my homemade knit dresses.

CHAPTER 13

The New York Sindrome

The scene opens with a skyline view of New York. The scene *always* opens with a skyline view of New York. This gives an immediate indication that what follows is going to be BIG BIG BIG.

If the scene opened with a view of Great Bend, Kansas, you'd know immediately that what was to follow was not going to be BIG. Some movies which have to take place in Great Bend, Kansas, open with a skyline view of New York before panning to Great Bend, just to show that this can be big, too.

But rest assured: you will never see a scene where the hero shakes his hand at the skyline and says, "I'll lick you yet, Great Bend, Kansas!" Almost anyone can beat Great Bend and if you live there, perhaps the best thing to do *is* to beat it.

If you live in New York, this is something quite different. You are constantly aware that everything around you is the biggest and the best. Even if it is not true. The only problem about New York's biggest and bestness is that you cannot brag about it to New Yorkers; they know it already and they will think you are from out of town. Even if they are from out of town.

The only thing to do, then, is to leave New York once in a while to get a new perspective and to have a chance to brag about New York. When you return, you can always take to saying, "It's a nice place to live, but I wouldn't want to visit." Most New Yorkers have visited places like Chicago and Baltimore and Phoenix and have not endeared themselves. Their reactions have given birth to a counterreaction, revealed in the expression, "New York is not America." It rankles the Chicagoans, for example, no end when network television commentators give detailed reports on New York weather and local news. Chicago is usually omitted or slighted. It nettles Los Angelinos (or is it Los Anglicans?) that their dreams for a New York on the West Coast have never quite materialized, even though their city is one-third New Yorkers and the rest are members of the L.A. County Police Department. The cold fact continues—the action is in New York and shows no signs of leaving.

When we say New York, we really mean, of course, the New York metropolitan area. This includes some 15,000,000 people or more. Since the area includes almost 10 per cent of the nation's population, it is easy to see that New York is both a trend setter and a major market. If something will sell well in New York, chances are it will do rather well in the rest of the country. However, just to play it safe, the advertising agencies and manufacturers invariably try out new products in places other than New

York to see if they will go well in New York. Then, these new products are brought into New York because if they go well in New York, they will go well out of New York.

The paradoxical thing about the big town is that its famed or infamous pace, its rapid rushing, is partly because the territory is a conglomeration of little towns, linked by a fantastic but crumbling transportation system. Masses of people troop back and forth to work daily in New York, underground, on the ground, in the water, under the water, and some even by air. We make a regular attempt to inform commuters of travel conditions during the course of our program—but this is a next to impossible task. The New York Metropolitan Area covers too much area. It concerns too many people. If all of the information that we have tells us that traveling conditions are normal, we are afraid to say so because the next minute may bring a commuter crisis. So we do the best thing there is to do: we tell the listeners that we are incompetent to deal with the problem. They are on their own.

The day will come, we believe, when all of the traffic information will be correlated, analyzed, and dispensed by intricate and omniscient computer machines. The information will be perfect and instantaneous. By that time, however, only machines will be going to work anyhow, so until that time the people in the New York Metropolitan Area will have to make do with information from idiots like us.

New York, despite its imperfections, is the only place in the United States where, without causing any commotion whatsoever, you can:

(1)   Walk around with a beard (this includes women)
(2)   Talk to yourself
(3)   Lie on the sidewalk
(4)   Get change in a drugstore without buying a candy bar
(5)   Ask a policeman something and have him answer, "I'm a stranger here myself."
(6)   Buy at least eight daily newspapers and not one of them in English
(7)   Always see someone you know when you don't want to see anyone you know
(8)   Always tell your spouse, "I was caught for two hours in a traffic jam."
(9)   Get away with anything

Conversely, New York is the only place in the United States where, without causing concern to anyone except yourself, you cannot:

(1)   Get anything done on just one phone call
(2)   Get crosstown
(3)   Ask directions of two people without starting a fight
(4)   Recognize a celebrity
(5)   Get anything for less than $3.98
(6)   Fight City Hall, because you can't find it
(7)   Find anybody who remembers who was mayor after Fiorello
(8)   Find anybody who, deep down, really likes the Yankees

(9) Get your size

(10) Get away with anything

There are numerous fallacies about New York which we would like to explode. If we can correct some of the mistaken impressions about New York, this whole book may be justified, but this is asking a great deal.

Fallacy: All New Yorkers are loud.

This is a rather difficult point to explain. New Yorkers are not loud; other people are too quiet. When you put eight million people in such a small area; when you operate immense machinery, millions of vehicles, millions of appliances, a million offices and factories, it tends to get rather noisy. In order to be heard above the din and roar of the surroundings, one must speak up. When a New Yorker goes elsewhere, the *absence* of sound makes him seem loud.

Fallacy: All New Yorkers are smart-alecky.

Untrue. These simple, lovable people are overexposed to publicity, overexploited by advertising, overpowered by surveys, overhung by overindulgence. They are underestimated by advertisers, underrated by movie and TV producers, under suspicion by the tourists, under surveillance by the FBI, and underground by the subways. It is just that they say, "Oh yeah?" a lot.

Fallacy: All New Yorkers were born on the Lower East Side.

Nothing could be further from the truth. Only rich and successful New Yorkers were born on the Lower East Side.

Fallacy: Manhattan Island was purchased from the Indians for $24 in beads.

This is not, in itself, a fallacy, however people are inclined to think of this price as inexpensive. The truth of the matter is, that if that same $24 in 1626 had been invested in AT&T stock (which was selling at $.02 a share and mighty shaky at that) the price of the island could better be considered at about $74,000,000. This price, mind you, was without running water.[1] The man who purchased New York was Peter Minuit who, everybody knows, really turned out to be William Zeckendorf.

Fallacy: New York is a summer festival.

Now, that *is* a fallacy.

So much for public service.

New York offers more for more people than any other place in America, but it costs more. According to figures leaked from the Department of Commerce, it is altogether impossible to live in New York on what you make unless you have a child acting in TV commercials and handle his or her money.

New York is a place which is busting at the seams, falling apart at the joints, and so disorganized it cannot last another ten years. And these facts are just as true today as they were when first said fifty years ago. It is a community that has so many anti-everythings and pro-everythings that

---

[1] Running Water, in turn, was sold to Chief Sitting Bull of the Sunbonnet Sioux.

they balance out, leaving only the people who don't care about anything to care about anything.

To prove the point, we would conclude this graphic picture of New York with quotes from unimpeachable sources:

"They'll never impeach me!"—Andrew Johnson

"New York is a nice place to live, but I'd rather live in Washington."—Governor Nelson Rockefeller

"Everyplace but New York is Perth Amboy."—Chamber of Commerce, Perth Amboy, N.J.

"A cleaner New York is up to you."—Chicago, Illinois

"I got my job through *The New York Times.*"—Editor, *New York Times*

"Grow old with me, the best is yet to come."—American Medical Association

CHAPTER 14

Schtick with the Bit

Each trade or profession has a language of its own. These are shorthand methods of talking which the participants use among themselves and sometimes to amuse or baffle outsiders. Perhaps you have heard your physician talking to his nurse about "doing an EKG." Maybe your doctor has remarked about the high rate of basal metabolism these days. Or possibly your doctor or dentist has given you a free sample of Anacin, which hardly fits the discussion but does show the power of radio advertising. Bakers have a language of their own, chefs have cooked up their own lingo. Even the butchers have their own tongue.

One interesting aspect of show-business talk is that frequently it is used more by sideline or marginal people than by the performers themselves. Finch and I rarely use showbiz language, possibly because we have difficulty enough being understood when we talk normally. But many others around us do use entertainment jargon. The following dramatization (all names are fictitious and many have been omitted or shortened out of fear) may illustrate:

The scene: Klavan and Finch, with their managers Arthur and Howard, await the arrival of John V. B. Sullivan, the radio station manager, who is due in for a contract discussion.

The K and F managers are attorneys, regular college graduates, who represent the team, as well as an assorted, long and impressive list of performers and writers. Arthur and Howard (both the Bar Association and the Diners' Club request that we omit their last names) represent Staunton Beachem, for one, the head electrician on *Sunset Strip;* Paul Singerfield, the teleprompter operator on the Coca-Cola commercials; Hyndley Walpole, keeper of the NBC peacock; and Shorts Carlysle, the house doctor during the six-year run of *My Fair Lady* who put himself through med school working over the fainters at Wednesday matinees. Of course, our managers represent other show business notables, but we have listed only the most prominent.

As they wait, standing around the fashionable Fifth Avenue lobby of WNEW, one flight up overlooking the magic-tricks-and-dirty-picture store, the receptionist is seen also. A tall, broad-shouldered, athletic individual, who looks a lot like Abraham Lincoln, she is in fact a southern girl. Arthur, one of the managers, starts to approach her.

Arthur is a man pushing fifty (behind him), a person who lives well, looks well, and dresses well on the blood money paid him by his clients. He is an associate of some of the biggest names in show business and has rubbed elbows for years at Lindy's during lunchtime. His sleeves show it. To be perfectly honest, Klavan and Finch rarely see Arthur, most of their business being handled by Howard. Arthur is usually involved in top-level conferences with network presidents, advertising agency brass, and two terrible race horses that have feigned death throughout the nation's less affluent race tracks.

Howard, on the other hand, handles most of the team's negotiations. This leaves him a good deal of time. He is an excellent athlete. One of his specialties is playing handball with older clients who have mentioned him in their wills. Howard hails from Kansas City, Missouri, a condition which he treats as some sort of deformity. He dresses in true showbiz style, conservatively, with black silk mohair suits, white shirts and white ties. Occasionally, he wears a white-on-white shirt which allows him to forego a tie since it looks like a white shirt with a white tie. Quickly described, Howard might be said to resemble a younger, hairier, darker, shorter Otto Preminger who resembles an older, fatter, shorter Yul Brynner. Yul Brynner and Howard, on the other hand, do not resemble each other at all.

As Arthur approaches the receptionist, she looks up and asks, politely, "Yeah Clyde? What's the gig?" She shows little awareness of who Arthur is, or even that she recognizes the fact that he is an attorney. This is especially difficult to ignore, inasmuch as Arthur wears his Bachelor of Laws degree sealed in plastic as a tie clip.

"Veratas Vos Liberabit," Arthur says with legal splendor. Howard, who is a man of action, appears at his partner's side to expedite matters. He grasps the receptionist

firmly by the bun of her hairdo and asks, "Sweetie, is The Man in?"

The receptionist, also a regular college type, puts both hands on his cheeks and responds: "Hold for four, Daddy-o, I'll pick up the horn and give him a shout." She puts Howard down on the floor again and rings for Mr. Sullivan's secretary. Soon, the boss's alluring secretary, Miss Zam, appears through the shoji screen to usher us into the front office. It is not before Miss Zam has kissed Arthur, Howard, Finch and myself that we infiltrate the palatial office from whence issue all memoranda.

The boss's office is like any other: gold carpet, gold furniture, gold hi-fi, emerald flag of Ireland and the ruby lips of Miss Zam. The boss is in the office looking even as he looks today: a good-looking man with silver temples, a red face, and an early-fortyish bounce accentuated by the fact that he wears a cashmere football jersey with the number 1130 on the back. (He has a spare cotton jersey with the number 102.7, the FM frequency, which he wears when being investigated by the FCC.) Sullivan, the boss, is a Dartmouth man and he inserts this fact into every conversation. This information may be harmless enough, but it is especially embarrassing when he does this at funerals. Of course, he is the boss.

Arthur shakes hands with Sullivan and says, *"Pugnam minificare."*

"Man," says Sullivan, greeting Arthur.

"Mother," Howard says, shaking Sullivan's hand.

"Babymine," responds Sullivan.

"Sir," Finch hisses, moving quietly to the couch.

"Talent," Sullivan answers.

"Hello, Mr. Sullivan," I say, extending my hand.

"Dartmouth four; Harvard three," Mr. Sullivan barks, ignoring my hand but graciously motioning me to sit next to Finch, out of the way.

Miss Zam stands next to Sullivan, her hand playfully engaging his jersey collar and occasionally massaging his neck.

"OK, cut!" the boss says to Miss Zam, "sign-off now and stand-by in case I need a fill." Miss Zam languorously leaves the office, blowing kisses.

The boss picks up the copy of the contract under consideration and riffles through the pages. He puts on a pair of heavy horn-rimmed glasses. The frame is engraved, "Anytime, anyplace, N E W." Then he looks squarely at Howard. "Howie, I ran through the bit with the chairman of the board on the thing, whatever."

"He dig?" Howard asks.

"Well," says Sullivan cagily, "he didn't flip over some of the lyrics but he said the melody seemed pretty easy to hum. He'll be here in five to talk about the thing and the thing and whatever."

"Nulle prosse, habeas corpus," Arthur replies, whipping out a foot-long cigarette holder with a blackened end. He has been told to give up cigarettes so he lights the holder. Smiling knowingly, he adds, *"Mandamus referendum."*

"Crazy, baby," Howie puts in just for laughs and we all do.

Miss Zam enters at this juncture to inquire whether we want a drink. She has changed from satin lounging pajamas into a low-cut, black silk dress. Her apparently normal blond hair is now concealed under a flaming red wig. She looks around the room dreamily. "Any of you cats for juice?"

"I'll have mine dark with one lump of sugar," I order suavely.

"She means hard stuff," Finch corrects, as he pinches Miss Zam.

"Not for me, darling," Howard adds. "We want to knock off this schtick before we break for chow."

Finch, sensing a lack of understanding, explains that "schtick" is a synonym for "bit" which is a synonym for a bit of business in a routine. Miss Zam understands everything and flounces out of the office with the message, "I'll reprise later unless you cue me in front." Miss Zam already looked pretty cued in front.

More studying of the contract by Sullivan ensues during which time he sings, almost imperceptibly, "Vo do dee oh, voom voom vo." In the backround I can hear Howard keeping time with "Voot voot, voot vootie." Finally, Sullivan looks up and appeals to Howard and Arthur, *"Look,* you're beginning to be hypoed by your own flack. We're an indie, not a syndie. Whatever bread we can scuff over and above the above and below the line put-out, we'll try to give you. But as an encore . . ."

"What's he saying?" I fairly shriek at Finch.

"Sh," Finch shh's, "I think we got him."

"E Nostra rebellio praemonere," Arthur mutters menacingly. He pulls a pocketbook edition of the New York Code of Laws Unexpurgated Vols 1–6 out of his bulgy

breast pocket. Luckily, at this point, where the conversation seems to be becoming unseemly, the shoeshineman comes in, carrying his small portable shinestand.

"Roadshow," says Sullivan.

"Run-off music," Howard adds.

"*Amo, amas, amat,*" Arthur enjoins.

"I'll have a shine too," I chirp. But Finch kicks me. The shineman has just been told to return at a more opportune moment. The seventy-five-year-old man, unperturbed, leaves doing a time-step and singing the love theme from *Cleopatra*.

"All right, Jack, let's take it from the top," Howard resumes. "Paragraph 1-A, how does that grab you?"

But the conversation is not destined to be resumed, for at this moment, Miss Zam returns, wearing a delightful Fiberglas peignoir and a lurid auburn wig with teased hair. She introduces into the sanctum the chairman of the board, followed by the corporation's research director, the vivacious Mrs. Zutty Feldman. They are followed by the chairman of the board's chauffeur.

The chauffeur sets up a canvas director's chair for the chairman and the chairman chairs. Mrs. Feldman expressively surveys the room and sinks to the carpet on her crossed expressive legs. Finally, the chairman of the board, who looks like a young Pat O'Brien or an old Nick Adams, speaks to his chauffeur. "Harley, exit stage left and see if you can pick up a couple of twofers, some hard ticket flick for Mrs. Chairman and myself." Harley, the chauffeur, a man of impressive military bearing, salutes and answers with the simple acquiescence: "Cha cha cha, leader man."

I never found out what it was that he was sent for, but I am happy in the knowledge that even Arthur, that old show business buss, is also quizzical. He whispers to Howard, *"Quo vadis?"*

Howard snaps back the answer, "Loved him; hated her." And all is still.

But the chairman is not one to waste time on social amenities. He proceeds with a vengeance to the contract. Ignoring Finch and myself completely, he makes his summation to Howard and Arthur. His message is both laudatory and critical.

"Jack has clued you," he says, "the two kooks do lootsville pretty good. But although we can't afford an AM spectacular we don't want to go dark or do the top forty bit. So, we'll take their Pulse, up the guarantee, raise the spot cut-off in exchange for exclusivity. Zutty has been swinging with the ratings and Mad Ave. and she'd better fill in the dialogue."

Finch turns and explains—it's good to work with an older man—what the chairman has said. (Translation: Mr. Sullivan has already informed you of our position. Klavan and Finch bring in a sizable amount of income. We cannot afford to pay for a gigantic morning show but we also do not desire to go off the air in the morning; nor do we desire to descend into the doldrums of the top-forty hit tunes. So, after we check their ratings on the Pulse rating service, we'll increase their guaranteed income by giving them a share of each commercial fee—up to a point. They must, in return, guarantee us that they'll appear nowhere else.)

"Does that mean we're fired?" I ask, but Finch puts his fist in my mouth because it is time to hear from Mrs. Feldman.

Mrs. Zutty Feldman suddenly rises and tugs at her form-fitting jumper. Her beautifully streaked black hair flies sexily over her face; she brushes it aside with an expressive gesture. She whips out a roll of charts with rating figures.

"Chartwise, the audience breakdown follows the profile forecast. Agency-wise, the spot pickup is consistent in short-term flights with long-termers and make-goods shaping out the log." Her black hair falls over her expressive dark eyes and the chairman of the board gallantly rushes from his chair to clear her forehead. She resumes: "Repeat biz is high and promos low. Adjacencies to news availabilities are short; quarter hour twenties are OK as long as they are ET's, timewise and buywise."

"Likewise, hey, hey," Howard says because obviously it is an optimistic situation. Then all of the men rush over and kiss Mrs. Zutty Feldman on her expressive, full lips and she sits down, blowing kisses to all, scattering charts every-where. As I reach over to pick up some of the charts, the chairman of the board regales us with small-talk before making his final offer. "I notice," he remarks solicitously, "that you two flips are spinning more Tony and Perry and less Bobby and Connie. I was gassin' the other day with Jackie and Julie. They said to cool the groove and lay on the uncool."

With no idea of what he was saying, I have no ready answer. But Finch, with that tremendous social sense of his, answers knowingly: "Bull!"

Arthur and Howard look at the contract again and confer in whispers. Their conversation is tense and punctuated by an occasional outburst from Howard. "I dig, Father-face, I dig." or "Aw man, don't put me down cause you bring me down when you put me down." I assume that they have to make a few changes which enable both sides to settle reasonably and quickly because they return the contract to Sullivan. Sullivan stops puckering at Zutty and the entire party shakes hands all around. Finch and I, for some reason, are ignored in all the hand-shaking and remain in our places. I take this opportunity to reclaim Mrs. Feldman's charts from the floor and return them to her. She kisses me expressively and says, "You're a Dickie Burton." I feel that this is good.

After what seems an interminable time, Arthur motions for us to come to the desk and sign the papers. He smiles and says, *"Caveat emptor."* It is foolish to try to read the document because Sullivan's hands cover the upper parts of the pages charmingly. "Cats," he says, "don't go Actors Studio on me; no rehearsal, you know all the lines." Afraid to delay him we signed quickly. The chairman of the board scrawls a dollar mark for his signature and starts out of the office. He looks over his shoulder and calls, "Got to cut serfs: got a bash with Frank, Dean, Joey, and Sammy, and the FCC." Leaving the office, he is unable to shake hands because he carries his folding chair with one hand and holds Mrs. Zutty Feldman's hand with the other. She too throws an expressive glance over her naked shoulder as she calls, "Happy Hoopers, and Big Billing!" It is a fun parting at that.

After we have all kissed Miss Zam, Howard, Arthur, Finch, and I leave the office and walk down the long green corridor to the station exit. We bid our managers goodbye, without kissing them, and we hear Howard going down the stairs singing, *"Nothing ever pays the rent/like the talents' ten per cent."*

I remain looking at Finch, the older partner. "How in the world did you, a normal, unshow-business type comprehend the tremendous badinage from the milieu of the show-business environment?" Finch looks at me, his visage all modesty. "Man, like I don't dig what you are saying," he answers.

CHAPTER 15

On the Double Talk

One of the gimmicks we have used on the air for years, and which seems invariably successful in getting a chuckle is double talk. Double talk is largely for laughs, but it also has its serious uses. To some of us, double talk is a way of life as important as Zen Buddhism or more sales. To others, it is a tremendously useful tool. If you have nothing to say, for example, but feel you must say something, use double talk. Double talk, in this sense, is next to wisdom. And wisdom is next to Denver.

Double talk is not only useful at home, where it is the vocal patois, especially in Washington and in New York, but it also can be entertaining abroad. If you're not entertaining a broad, you will find that it is useful in Europe. If you can do double talk with a French accent, you'll amuse a Frenchman. If you can do double talk with an Italian accent, you'll amuse an Italian. If you have no desire to amuse either Italians or Frenchmen, it is better to eat only in Chinese restaurants.

I remember an occasion in the Hotel Hassler—a fine place in Rome, next to the Spanish Steps (or is it in Spain, next to the Roman steps?[1])—when Finch and I, speaking double talk, succeeded in convincing a bartender that we were an Egyptian archaeological team intent on excavating the Colosseum and moving it 4000 feet closer to the Forum. Such a feat had, of course, previously been considered an impossibility. Not moving the Colosseum; convincing the bartender. But Finch is good with bartenders. He spent a great many of his formative years under their care. Yet it was the double talk that did it.

The following short course in double talk is designed to allow anyone to speak meaningless nonsense with great import. Many people do that without speaking double talk but at least with double talk it *sounds* as if you are saying something. Speaking double talk fluidly can be a boon in business and a splendid aid in relations with the opposite sex. If you have no desire to commit yourself on a certain subject, throw in a little double talk and your opinion will remain safe forever in your own tortured mind. At a meeting of the staff, when you are called upon to utter some deep, cogent opinion on a matter which could well dissolve your whole way of life, how simple to stand up before

[1] Many people are confused by the difference between *accents* and *dialects*. Dialects, scholars, including me, tell us, refer to differences between pronunciation of different regions within the same country. Accents, on the other hand, are differences in pronunciation among people from different countries. Or vice versa. This is easily remembered by the use of a simple memory device. I always keep it in mind by thinking to myself: *A*ccents *a*ther countries. *Di*alects mean *di*s country. Try not to forget this simple memory device. If you should be unable to produce it, or if you should lose this page, one good place to look is in Rome, next to the Spanish Steps.

everyone and say significantly: "The problem is one of relative simplicity, if you take the right corvin of it. I would simply rout the mintons by the deskut and wern the shaubles." This kind of comment will transfix any vice-president, at least until the next staff meeting by which time you will be able to teach your spouse a trade.

Perhaps your current romantic interest is intent on receiving a definite answer to that time-worn question "Do you love me?" It is far from entangling to answer with a look of warmth and affection, "Darling, would I trolig and kert with you if I didn't have the utmost permis for you?" This, delivered breathlessly but with effective simplicity, should keep from lousing up a good thing for at least another month.

By this time, several obvious facets (a real word) of double talk should be evident and it should be reassuring to know that you can learn double talk if you will observe a few essentials.

(1) Keep your double talk words short. A longer word allows your listener to really listen and realize that it is *you* who are out of your mind. A ferb is far better than a krilisbornigspan.

(2) Don't overdo it. People are usually only listening to be polite so that they may start talking. If they hear too much that they don't comprehend, they will forget what they are going to say and ask you to repeat. Repetition of double talk, like repetition of magic tricks, is all-revealing.

(3) Make your double-talk syllables sound like real syllables. Add just a letter to a real word and you can

baffle even the most intellectual listener. For example: strare, aclarity, shearse, chaggle. Who would dare question the statement "I'd *love* to see you today, Charlie, but I'm seeing my lawyer about the possiblity of a large derosion."

(4) Use actual words in an incorrect application. In other words, stick a legitimate word in a place where it doesn't belong. More succinctly, add a bird to your map. If you do this carefully, you can become a real person of mystery in any crowd. When some ill-meaning, nosy neighbor asks "Didn't I see you with Cynthia Jones at the track yesterday?" you can answer "You couldn't have seen me. I was having my burning bush threaded at the top of the pane starters." For all Mr. Nosy knows now, you really were having your burning bush threaded.

(Phase II)

You have moved with such dispatch through the first phase, you are ready to become two-phased and apply advanced principles to the beauty and science of living. Hasn't it always been a thorn in your side to meet the hyperintellectual chap at a party—the man who has done, read, and seen everything? How many times have you thirsted to turn to a conversational monopolist and shatter him with a well-chosen ad-lib? Double talk makes all such dreams reality. If you are not sure of yourself, we advise memorizing a few simple seemingly off-the-cuff bon mots. (Another secret in using this weapon of destruction is to throw the line and then get out.)

Example: Your antagonist is discoursing at length about the inadequacies of the administration. He is obviously well informed, well read, and prepared for any argument. You turn, look him straight in his beady eyes, and say with great strength: "Admitting part of your postulate, doesn't it seem to you that the Kennedy group shows a great deal more bendrusting that the previous crate? And if you admit *that,* how about the starbars?" Immediately after you have made a stand, turn to the other guests for approval and say triumphantly, "Hah! Isn't that a blister?" Then run off to refill your drink.

If your drink does not need refilling when you start talking, empty your glass into your purse or your trouser cuff. If there is no escape and your fellow debater answers you (he may be drunk and think he understands) stand where you are and retort with this comment: "That's all right for you to craulb, but you're prejudiced because of last year's motor nine."

If you still find it impossible to edge to the bar, fall down on the floor and yell, "Harb! Harb! It's my harb!" This little device will give you time for a delaying action and possibly a grand slam by making everyone think your sparring partner has shoved you. As a final protective measure it would be wise to arrange to acquire a new set of acquaintances if you are one of those people to whom friends are important.

Thinking positively, one need never go to college or read voraciously to obtain a reputation for having gone to college or reading voraciously. One merely sprinkles one's conversation liberally with pure double-talk quotations. Let us put you in an untenable position: You are a young person on a cruise ship looking for casual, friendly companionship and a chance to be supported forever. You realize that you are near a catch but you also soon realize that you are in deep water. This calls for cultural embellishment. You look long and deeply into the sea, pause a moment and then say, "Wasn't it Shakespeare"—not a doubletalk word—"who said, 'Show me the sea, and I'll show thee a flars. Show me a flars and I'll eat dortin forever.'" Then smile and pucker your lips to be kissed. If that certain someone is not receptive by now, it might be well to threaten to jump overboard. You can use this quote: "Goodbye cruel world, life is a dancher draulm and I—I am not prone to rish." If that certain someone doesn't dive in after you, then the hell with it; life really is a dancher draulm.

Finally, remember that double talk was originally used as a substitute for those common, ordinary, four-letter words that were heard around the house. Examples of everyday epithets which were once double talk are: Dagnab it! Darn! Flub. Basset. Since, as good Americans, we are always trying to improve our vocabularies, let us add a few brand-new words which can gain recognition eventually on their own. (Remember: learn a word a day, and by this time next year no one will be able to understand you. Then you can run for public office.) Try these: Dasabbit! You barndangger! That dirty little firmbinder!"

Picture the scene as the boss approaches you on a Monday morning. Seething with contempt because you have goofed an order, he cries: "Jones, what the hell did you *do* with this order?"

You take the paper and look at it. You do not recognize it but it obviously came past your desk. You say hopefully: "Good heavens, sir, this traf should have been deployed last wink. If it weren't for that little fich Morty Smith, this grab would never have hammed."

"Are you calling my brother's boy Morton a fich?" the boss screams incredulously. Now you fight to regain your composure, having discovered that your assistant is the boss's nephew. This is a fact you could hardly be expected to know since you are rarely in the office. But double talk sees you through, you reply with complete confidence, "Yessir, if Morty weren't such an accomplished baln, this order would never have ringed. He's a real fich, that kid!"

Smiling, placated, and amiable, the boss leaves muttering, "After all, my brother is a real go-getter, too. I guess little Morty *is* just a son of a fich."

SUGGESTED READINGS ON DOUBLE TALK:

Das Kapital—the Marx Brothers
A' Roman on the Spanish Steps—Franz Kafka
We Die At Dawn—Klavan
Selected correspondence between the Soviet and Chinese People's Republic Heads of State

CHAPTER 16

Finch and the Big Time

If your otherwise normal son or daughter evinces an early interest in show business, radio or television, there are only two things you can do: ignore the little blighter until the neighborhood kids destroy him or become a stage parent. Since stage parents are probably worth a volume or two themselves, and by qualified medical authorities at that, let us consider the alternative solution: ignore the offspring. That is exactly what happened in the case of young Durwood Finch of Binghamton, New York.

When young Durwood, who was destined to distinguish himself later by becoming my partner, went to his mother and informed her that he wanted to become a radio announcer, she ignored him at first. After all, it was not so very long before that fateful day when he had told her that he wanted to be a horse-drawn milk wagon. Another possible reason for ignoring her son was Mother Finch's lack of understanding as to just what was a radio announcer? This situation would be comparable to your child coming home to you and announcing that he wanted to be an electronic pipefitter on the Nova project. To this very day,

Finch remembers his mother's reply to the startling use of the words "radio announcer." She dropped the ladle with which she had been stirring the apples for the applejack and slapped him full across his cupid bow's mouth. "Don't ever use words like that around this house again!" she shrieked, terrified lest his two sisters be contaminated in their relationship with men.

It was a far cry, too, from the interest Finch had shown in amateur radio, to commercial radio, that burgeoning but mystical means of communication which had so recently happened upon the scene. It was one thing to yell "Calling CQ, Calling CQ" into a radio ham transmitter but quite another to sell the services of the Parlor City Shoe Company, where one mispronunciation could put an announcer out of business forever.

To humor Dee, he was allowed to work with an uncle who had the loudspeaker concession at the *George F.* pavilion in nearby Johnson City. Dee became the announcer on the loudspeaker who introduced the famed orchestras of the day—Jean Goldkette, Husk O'Hare, and Ozzie Nelson—and announced the license numbers of drivers who had blocked the driveway with their horse and buggies. Through the last years of high school, he worked at night handling the announcing chores at the pavilion while the teenagers of that tortured era did the shag, the Lindy, the jitterbug and all the terrible things that we swear to our teenagers we never did. In his last year at Binghamton High, he even landed on the local radio station WNBF as a part-time announcer. Finch was president of his senior class at Binghamton High but because of a run-in with a teacher he did not appear on the stage at graduation. He had evidently given the teacher his rather prejudiced opinion of the teacher's capabilites and was almost expelled from school. A simple apology would have reinstated him to the exalted position as class leader; but Finch refused, preferring to watch his class's graduation from the balcony of the auditorium while he chattered away, magpielike, with derogatory remarks about all concerned.

His formal education complete, Finch began full-time employment at WNBF as an honest-to-goodness radio announcer. Until 1939, he was employed there, handling the many jobs that an announcer at a local station must do: newscasting, introductions to religious shows and foreign language broadcasts, bible readings, MC work, disc jockeying, and cleaning up the studios. It was only after four years at WNBF that Finch was free to look for another job.

The station was located in a local hotel wherein standard social functions took place. It happened, after a particularly ornate affair in the hotel's ballroom, there was a superfluity of beer, left over in the form of untapped kegs. One of the bellhops assured Finch and another announcer that for $5.00, a keg of beer would be theirs. Since the beer was not the bellhop's to sell, Finch and his co-worker spirited the spirits out of the men's room window, congratulating themselves on a job well done.

Unfortunately, in removing the beer to a lakeside retreat belonging to the family of the future Mrs. Finch, the beer somehow went sour. Five dollars of ill-gotten gain went into the lake. More unfortunate was the fact that the owner of the beer had counted the kegs. The police of Binghamton, who were not so occupied at the time as they must be today, deduced from beating on the bellhop that the beer could only have gone to a couple of them no-account, consarned radio announcer fellas. The bellhop and the two no-accounts went bouncing into the ranks of the unemployed. Finch and his co-worker are still in the radio business, but the bellhop has gone on to other accomplishments. He is today one of the largest discount beer salesmen in the East.

Finch was forced out into the world beyond Binghamton; that writhing, fierce scrounging world where all is not right and the Susquehanna River does not carry the garbage off into the Chesapeake Bay. Finch gained employment at station WAGE in Syracuse, New York, over a hundred miles away. For a year he worked in the big town, acquiring poise, stature, elegance and learning how to buy cold beer by the hot keg without getting caught. There was something about Syracuse that made him seek the bigger time. Although he auditioned successfully in Philadelphia; he inexplicably rejected the job when it was offered. Somehow he saw Philadelphia as two Syracuses—and half a Binghamton. Subcutaneously,[1] he felt the draw of New York and he knew that the itch could not go unscratched. In radio, New York was headquarters and there was no place to go but New York if one were to enter the really top echelon of broadcasting.

Finch bade his time until his first two-week vacation,

---

[1] From Cole Porter's "I've Got You Under My Skin."

cleaned out his drawer of the filing cabinet, and prepared
to depart. So sure of himself and his future was he, that
he told the other announcers at WAGE that he was off to
the big time and would not be back. Since all announcers
everywhere once dreamed of working in New York, it
would have been only natural that the other voices of
WAGE would have staged a large celebration for their de-
parting hero. But humanity being what it is, the only comments were: "Where's the five dollars?" "Can I have your
filing cabinet drawer?" and "Listen to him, a reggalar
Graham MacNamee!"

To his wife, Finch left the message that he would be
sending for her in a few days; they were moving to New
York. Mrs. Finch, a fearless little girl from a minor town,
was clever enough to suspect desertion and therefore did
not give up her job as teacher in a posh private school for
boys. She did, however, engage the services of a nefarious
Syracuse lawyer, on a standby basis, in case Finch and romance faded away. She need not have feared.

Dee arrived in New York ready to accept the job that
he was sure was waiting. Of course, it had to be the right
thing—something with a salary. His surprise was considerable when he found after auditioning at one of the networks that there was no opening. The network executives
were very interested in him, in his style of announcing and
his potentiality. They were momentarily expecting an important call, however, because they told Finch not to call
them they would call *him*. Having nothing else to do
while waiting for the call, Finch auditioned at what was
then the Blue Network. The first network had apparently

forewarned the Blue Network that Finch was their property because the Blue Boys evinced no interest in him at all. A day passed. Finch was becoming a trifle hysterical; didn't New York know what was going on? Did not the vast broadcasting clique realize that he was there? He stopped in at the independent little radio station WNEW to audition while waiting for a bus. The year was 1941, a year that will live in infamy. Independent little WNEW heard Finch read the audition copy which consisted of 231 foreign names, a five-minute newscast, and a commercial for the plain pipe racks of Robert Hall.

Bernice Judis, the manager of the station, heard the audition as it progressed and wept just a little as she saw he was just a neophyte. She offered $45 a week. The neophyte wept as he accepted and left the building waving tearfully, just in time to make the bus. He was glad that he had the courage to accept the first job offered to him. But then, after all, he was armed with cockiness and the $5.00 he owed the announcer in Syracuse. After consulting a pocket dictionary, he was glad to find out that neophyte did not mean what he thought it did.

Dee sent a telegram to Mrs. Finch which said tersely: GOT IT. STOP. A lesser lady might have wondered what it was he had got and what she was to stop. But Betty knew what had happened and she dismissed her attorney. Armed with Dee's tremendous increase in salary, Betty Finch was able to resign her position at the posh boys school, thank Mr. Posh, and moved to New York to begin the good life at the fountain of money. If $45 a week doesn't sound like a great deal of money for a big New York announcer to make in 1941, remember, it wasn't. But when you have been working in Syracuse for less money and the less is the most you can make in Syracuse, then it is propitious to leave Syracuse. Besides, there was that five dollars which made it propitious to leave Syracuse, too. In addition, it is generally propitious to leave Syracuse.

Radio in 1941 was in its thriving, explosive heyday. If you can picture a world without TV and Telstar, and picture an America where Major Bowes, Artie Shaw, and Boake Carter were the daily topics of conversation, you have radio of 1941. The work itself was exciting and the programs were the result of superlative creativity. Finch was swept up in WNEW's routine of trying to compete against the vast network juggernauts with low budget and local enterprise. It was a stimulating life and it lasted for one whole year. In 1942 Dee was making $75 a week. He loved his work. He loved working at WNEW so much that it was a pitiful sight to see the MP's dragging him off to help a country that needed him so much less than the station.

Dee Finch served his country with the U. S. Army until 1946. For descriptions of his combat experiences, may we refer you to:

From Here to Eternity	— James Jones
The Young Lions	— Irwin Shaw
The Naked and the Dead	— Norman Mailer
CATCH 22	— Joseph Heller

World War II having been concluded successfully for our side, or so it seemed at the time, Finch returned to WNEW. The station had gained a certain prestige and eminence during the war years. It had developed the ability to give immediacy to the news and special events without the red tape ensnarling bigger operations. Finch found that the station had an alertness and a feeling of going places. He blossomed as announcer and MC, newscaster, and all-purpose voice (or mouth) of WNEW. Then came the blow which threatened to destroy everything.

The Finches were on vacation when a call came that Finch was needed immediately at WNEW. He was called back to fill in for Jack Lescoulie, one half of the morning team of Jack and Gene. Repeat: a morning team. Finch loved the night life of New York or anyplace. He loved the cup that cheers, lifting a toast with his wife, friends, neighbors, anybody on the street who could lift a cup. Now, for this interlude, he was going to have to get up early. He contemplated developing morning sickness. Instead, he railed on the air. He complained on the program to his temporary partner, Gene Rayburn, blaming the station, the audience, the government, and Stalin.[2]

The peculiar result was that the audience loved this approach to morning radio. They hated to get up early too. They liked to stay awake at night, scratchin' and laughin', and here was a chap who understood them. Finch remained on the morning program with Rayburn, complaining most of the time.

[2] "Stalin" was Joseph Stalin whose name and face have been erased from history by his successor, what's-his-name.

It was Rayburn who finally left. In 1952, both members of the team had reached a point where they were among the biggest names in radio in New York. They had done two network programs, one for CBS and one for ABC. Rayburn decided to try for television as well as radio; Finch decided to try to stay in radio. By this time, Finch could not understand why anyone would want to go into television where one had to stay up late at night and get up late in the morning. So Rayburn left for a competing position on NBC in New York. Finch was forced to seek a new partner.

WNEW and Finch auditioned scores of applicants for the replacement position. From among the 200 or more names suggested, one man's voice and talent constantly flashed above the others. One man kept coming before their minds as they listened and looked. One man, Gene Klavan, kept soaring above the others, forcing them to turn back to his audition record again and again. There was no denying that Gene Klavan was the man they would have to pick. So WNEW and Dee Finch reached down into the nation's capital and brought Gene Klavan in to help them out of their distress.

But enough talk about them, let's talk about me.

CHAPTER 17

Klavan and the Big Finch

"I guess some people like it," my father used to say after listening to the Klavan and Finch program, "but I can't see anything to it." Let me add that my father was a very intelligent man. I was working with Finch for five years before my father ceased harping on his favorite advice, "Why don't you go back to law school?"

During my last year in high school I studied public speaking because I was under the impression that it was easier than home economics. The name of the high school was the Baltimore City College, which may give you some clue as to how things are in Baltimore. That year in high school, I somehow became embroiled in part-time radio for the Board of Education, frequently appearing as a dying old man and a dying young man. Things haven't changed.

When high school was over, I sidled up to the director of radio work and asked her what she thought of radio as a career. "What else did you have in mind?" she asked charily.

"Well," I answered, just as warily, "I had thought of going to law school." With an audible sigh of relief, she said, "Well, I think that radio is overcrowded. Maybe you had

just better go in for The Law." The facts have later proved
that it was The Law, not radio, that was overcrowded.

I finished a pre-law course at Johns Hopkins University
which entitled me to pass Go and move directly to the University of Maryland Law School. It was 1942, and I began
on the accelerated wartime system. Everything was paced
so fast that you could be disbarred before you were gradu-
ated. I was one third of the freshman class of the Law
School. At the end of six months, we wound up in the following manner: one chap joined the Navy, one went insane, and I, having learned a lot from both, joined the
Army.

At the end of the war (the same war that gave us the
ever-popular song "Lilli Marlene") I found myself some-
where in the Pacific with a B-29 group. After VJ-Day, Special Services found me there too and I was placed in a
show called *Bedtime Stories for Adults*. General Curtis Le-
May may have been a great general, but he was a lousy
father-image.

In an impulsive moment, I had submitted a sheaf of material to *Esquire* magazine. The editors had the Machiavel-
lian sense of humor to pass it along to *Coronet* magazine,
their tax loss. Subsequently, I found myself working as an
assistant editor of *Coronet* in Chicago in 1946. That is not
quite true, I never really found myself. In fact, the reason
I had to leave *Coronet* was that I never could come out
even—I always lasted longer than my paycheck. When I
told the associate editor, Sey Chassler,[1] that I had to have

[1] Sey Chassler is currently executive editor of *Redbook*. He's all
right if you like talented, brilliant people who have made it on
their own. Personally, I can't stand the type.

more than $40 a week, he asked me what else I had in mind as a future because the magazine and radio business were overcrowded. He suggested that I try law school.

In May of 1947, I became an announcer/writer/newsman at WCBM, a small station in Baltimore. I had applied to this station armed with a sure-fire gimmik. Having heard one of their announcers on the air, it occurred to me that if *he* could be on the air, so could I. "If *that* announcer can be on the air," I was going to tell the program director, "so can I!" A rather distressing problem arose when the program director turned out to be *that* announcer. I thus received my first lesson in the quick-recovery ad-lib by fearlessly saying, "Oh . . ." Somehow, they hired me anyway, my first real radio job in my own hometown. They say that charity begins in your own hometown.

I must admit that I *had* to leave WCBM. I was doing so well there that I had been given the morning program. I guess I was a star, if that is possible at $63 a week. A piece of chicanery in collusion with a friend had put me in a rather embarrassing position.

I had received a call from Al Ross, the morning man at WBAL, asking me if I were interested in working the afternoon show at that large successful station. My instructions were to come to WBAL and hide in a basement waiting room so that no one was aware that one station was pirating a performer from another local station. Unfortunately, when I received the word to come to the program director's office, I was so enthusiastic that I ran, slipped, and fell *up* a flight of stairs and broke my ankle.

I remember, as I was carried out on a stretcher, looking

up into the faces of every employee and visitor of that station. The ankle did hurt a little, but I received a tremendous ovation on my way to the ambulance.

When I returned to WCBM, they had apparently become suspicious about my mishap, refusing to believe that I had fallen while teaching base running to Little Leaguers. I was informed that I was no longer doing the morning show; I was to be the announcer on the Polish and Czechoslovakian Hours.

I did not fall up or down the stairs of WITH in Baltimore, but I did work there for two years until 1949. In that year, I made a tremendous prognostication. I foresaw that radio was dead and that undoubtedly, on its ashes, television would rise to unpredictable artistic heights. Apparently, I was wrong on both counts. Nevertheless, I left WITH and went to WAAM Television in Baltimore. If you have ever joined a new organization, you will recognize that I made a fatal mistake immediately. I told the people at WAAM that I knew nothing about television, but that I was eager to learn. Six weeks later, I had apparently learned all they could teach me and I was out of a job.

WTOP Radio, Washington, D.C., put me on the air to keep the station open from 12:30 A.M. to 2 A.M. because it was cheaper than having a doorkey made. The only time previous that the station had remained on the air so late was with a chap named Arthur Godfrey, but he had turned ungrateful and gone on to the big time.

Washington, D.C., is not a late-night town. Nestled deep on the banks of the Federal Reserve between the Old Guard and the New Frontier, it is the kind of place where everybody goes to bed early, at the same time, so he can get up in time for rush hour. After all, everybody works for the same company.

Largely through the efforts of a man with the incredible name of Cody Pfansteihl, the WTOP publicity man, a creeping awareness began to circulate that WTOP was still on the air after midnight. He made certain that I appeared and was seen at the right places: supermarkets, theaters, raids, protest meetings against the DAR. In 1950 the program called—I'm ashamed to say—"Capitol Punishment" went on television as well as FM radio in what was called a "triplecast." This event gave me the fortuity to be three times as bad at the same time. I seized the opportunity.

With the exception of the newscaster, I was the only person on the program for an hour and a half and yet every television set that was on, was tuned to that program. It was the only program on.

By 1952 I was doing a TV program in Baltimore and one in Philadelphia in addition to the WTOP extravaganza. I was also the Mayor of Happy Town, an early CBS-TV children's show which had to be seen to be believed. And after many people saw it, they were still taking bets.

WTOP was partially owned by CBS and the place, consequently, abounded with newsmen, some of whom went on to greater things. I worked with Walter Cronkite, Eric Sevareid, Lou Cioffi, Ron Cochran, and Irving Zimmerman. Irving Zimmerman eventually went on to open a children's ready-to-wear store in Arlington, Virginia, and became very successful. I have no idea what happened to the other fellows. But that's showbiz.

After three years, in 1952, it was time to leave WTOP. I wouldn't like to make the statement that the manager of that station was an unfair taskmaster, but his favorite employment agency when he needed employees was Hertz-Rent-A-Slave. It was certainly not a matter of money that made me decide to leave because money was neither discussed nor given. It was not working conditions at WTOP, notwithstanding the fact that our program literally originated from a garage. On nights when the mobile unit was out, our studio was so vast it looked like a spectacular. On nights when the mobile unit was parked in the garage, it merely looked like the program came from a garage. It was sort of an early "Truck 54 Where Are You?"

Factually, I had received an offer to move to New York and television station WPIX. "At last," I said to myself, "New York!" This must have been some kind of a turning point—especially if I was talking to myself. The only thing remaining was a series of contractual discussions with WPIX.

Coincidentally, I received a call from Bruno Zirato, Jr., of CBS who claimed to be a friend of a man named Dee Finch. (If he had recommended me to Finch, says Finch, he was no friend.) I went to WNEW, met Finch, and auditioned. For some unfathomable reason, our audition went well and I was offered the job of replacing Finch's partner.

Faced with a choice of radio and TV, I decided to make the choice radio because if you die on radio, no one sees you go. If you die on TV, you perish in the full bloom of camera and lights. Perhaps mine is not an optimistic attitude but pessimists, at least, are never disappointed.

A series of clandestine meetings was arranged at the Park Avenue apartment of the WNEW station manager, Bernice Judis. Miss Judis was largely responsible for the music and news format which allowed radio to live on in a country that went TV-crazy shortly after the war. She was responsible for innumerable innovations in broadcasting and she was as wise in the ways of show business as anyone we have met. She provided for a week of dry-runs, a week where we would be doing the show under every actual condition except that of being on the air. But I fooled everybody. I appeared with a mammoth case of laryngitis for the entire week.

We never did rehearse. We never prepared anything. We just went on the air November 17, 1952. I am still not sure it worked out all right but we are still on the air— as of this writing—well over a hundred and fifty thousand commercials later.

Probably if we had had that first week of rehearsal, we would never have become a team because we surely would have discovered in that one week what it has taken us years to find out, that we are not going to make it.

I do know this, however,—the first six weeks were impossible. Every morning when we finished our stint on the air, I walked out of that studio with the distinct impression that I could never go back the next day. I do believe that Finch had the same gnawing feeling that he had made a terrible mistake.

Several catalysts kept the situation together. One was the

presence of our newscaster, the late Henry Walden. He took me aside one morning as I was tearfully packing my carpetbag, never to return. He explained the facts of life to me and told me that being a team member is like a marriage. You have to have trust and confidence and, uppermost, honesty. So I unpacked Finch's electric razor, his collection of Husk O'Hare records and his autographed picture of the 1939 World's Fair.

The other catalyst was my wife. It was the first time—for us—that this radio business had shown any real promise, any indication that an entire family could stay in one place and be almost like real people: having trouble with the landlord, running up excessive charge accounts, having psychological problems with the children—all the things that make a house a home.

In addition, I think she knew that I could never pass Law School.

(You may not have noticed this, but this chapter is eight pages long. I could have gone into greater detail with spectacular hilarity and huge entertainment. However, the chapter on Finch is nine pages long, we are a team and I am nothing if not generous. . . .)

CHAPTER 18

A Critique on Critics

WARNING: When any human being decides to get up and perform before other human beings, especially to make a living, he may be under the impression that he is asking for a pat on the back. In reality, he is also asking for a kick in the stomach. Anytime you put yourself on a pedestal, even if that pedestal is a stage, you invite people to knock you off. This statement is an essential part of the Klavan and Finch philosophy. There are other statements in our philosophy—you might even say cliché's—but this one, together with two others ("rub don't blot" and "everybody talks about the weather but the weather girl gets paid for it") are essential.

Why a kick in the stomach? For the simple reason that the critic, the professional critic, looms large in the life of most performers. Often after doing a show, there are moments when the performer asks himself why he did not learn a useful trade. As some kind of emollient to his ego, the performer often builds a mental picture of the sort of person he thinks the critic really is.

The performer begins to envision the critic at work,

presumably in his home environment. This fantasy that the performer constructs makes his own work more palatable and helps reduce his fears.

Perhaps letting you in on our conception of the home life of a critic would be a useful contribution. The sketch that follows represents no critic in particular, but in particulars, it is all of them.

Christopher Critic is awakened by his wife at about 1 P.M. She enters the bedroom of their New York apartment, which is furnished in terrible taste (his) and says, "Do you know what time it is?"

"I know everything," he says, yawning. The critic shoves the empty champagne bottles aside and screams for his breakfast.

"A moment, sir!" the harried woman responds. She sets down her two baskets of wash and runs out of the bedroom to draw his mudbath. Then, trying to hide the patches on her dingy skirt, she throws confetti at him and races back to the kitchen.

"You are Everyman!" she shouts, over her shoulder. Chris Critic stands in front of the medicine cabinet. He admires his fangs, and slowly, methodically, files each to a suitable point for the day's work. He finishes his bath, sets his hair, and dresses amidst the flowers and candy which eager performers, composers, and authors have sent him from around the world.

The bedroom contains a TV set for each channel and a radio for each station. All are going simultaneously.

"Trash, trash," he mutters, leaving the bedroom for the

breakfast nook. As he passes his two wan little children, he gives each a good-natured cuffing about the ears. Then he sits down to the morning meal.

"Are the eggs satisfactory, sir?" his wife asks. Her careworn face pleads for assent.

". . . lacking in taste and imagination," he answers, "a disaster."

"Perhaps the coffee, sir; perhaps the buns?"

"Although the ingredients for this breakfast were tastefully chosen, the lack of direction, the amateur production of the end product are characteristic of the untried, the disintegration in this country of the lost arts and skills of craftsmanship," he says, pushing the table out of the window. There is a silence before the crash as it strikes the ground, twenty-one stories below. His harassed wife, wincing, frightened almost beyond the power of speech, curtsies once more and asks, "Did you sleep well?"

"Sleep? With those damn lumps in the mattress?"

"Oh, sir—I forgot. Those were the piles of free tickets to plays and movies that came in yesterday. There might have been a carton or two of goodies from the networks but those were at the foot of the bed."

"Quiet, you slut!" Critic shouts. The woman is swaying with vertigo induced by fear. "Your grammar's bad and your syntax surfeits me with ennui." He washes out his mouth with coffee, spits it out and dissolves a large hole in the floor.

Pacified, he begins a joke. "There was this woman and her baby who embarked on a train ride for Philadelphia.

A man sat down next to them and said, 'That's an ugly baby you have there, lady . . .'"

"The fellow on the 'Tonight' show told that joke last night," his wife reminds him.

"That abysmal no-talent?" the critic screams. "I am more talented than that little snit will ever be."

"But he's the biggest thing in the country, even though he gets dirty now and then. You said so yourself in your column," his trembling wife murmurs.

The critic suddenly begins to weep into his gold lamé cuff. "Oh, why doesn't anyone discover what a great comedian I am?"

"I thought you were a dramatic actor," his wife remarks softly.

"That too."

"And MC?"

"Of course."

"And ballad singer?"

"Yes," Chris replies steadfastly, "and satiric impressionist and folk singer and adagio dancer!"

His wife looks at him in the spell of wonder, shocked at his new liberal attitude in allowing her to question him. She pursues it further, "Then why don't you do these things?"

Chris rises to his feet, "Because greater than all my talents is my magnificent capacity to *hate!* I have a hate that in itself is a thing of beauty; a thrashing, severing, consuming, exquisite hate that must be shared with all the world."

"Oh, how impressive," Mrs. Critic says and falls to her knees sobbing. She lies there crumpled.

Contemplating serenely the spasm-wracked body of his wife, the critic thoughtfully analyzes her posture. "Good show!" he shouts. "You're either doing Kim Hunter or Eileen Heckart. Right?" But the wife, unable to answer, merely continues to sob and whimper.

"There's a little Joanne Woodward in there, too," the critic says, wearying of the whole exhibition. He walks away and turns on the three TV sets and two transistor radios in the living room. Then the critic's daughter, a slight girl in tattered clothes clutching a new doll that is being featured on television, approaches him cautiously. The father relaxes for a moment. He asks in enticing tones, "Cinderella, I've been meaning to ask. What did you think of the Mickey Mouse Club yesterday?"

"Oh, Sir Father, I thought it . . . enchanting . . . fun for the kids. A must-see," she answers brightly.

"Ask a child if she likes a children's program. What stupidity! Are we going to let our children determine the future?" he remarks to himself. Then he continues, "If we are not careful, the world will be one giant Disneyland!"

"Oh, how glorious . . . fun for the kids . . ." Cinderella squeals.

"Out, out, you addict," he screeches at his daughter. Then he beckons her, "Send in Tiny Tim, I want to see him." The shivering child, doll in arms, scampers off.

Timothy Critic arrives with a hugh plastic submarine still in the box. An obviously prized possession, the submarine has a bold citation on the side of the box: *Every boy wants a Remco Toy and girls too.*

"Gee, Dad, sir, what do you desire? You beat me already today." The critic smiles benignly and puts his long nails on the bumpy top of his offspring's head. "Son, son," the father sneers, "Daddy won't hurt you." Then grabbing the child by the hair, he places his face close to the terrified little one and breathes, "Tim, my boy, did you sneak out like Daddy told you and play with the performers' children?"

"Yes, sir, Dad, yes," Tiny Tim yelps in pain.

"Good, good! Now, you have your daily quota of little dirties about them, things about their home lives only their families could know?" He pauses long enough to kick at the family dog.

"Yes, Dad Sir," the boy manages to say, "I never fail. When I grow up I want to be like you, rotten clean through!" He hands his father several grubby sheets of paper with notes scrawled on them.

"Four Stars! That's my boy," Chris says pushing his boy out of the room.

The critic then proceeds to erect a huge panel on which he pastes the pictures of the top ten show business personalities of the month. Playing the bongoes with one hand, he commences to throw darts at the pictures in tempo to the drumbeats. He sings a catchy little tune:

> Crush, ruin, kill, hate
> Shatter, break, annihilate
> Loathe, smash, eradicate
> I love me, cha cha cha.

At the end of the song, the unsmiling applause of the rest of the family comes from the hallway beyond. Chris Critic notices that the mother has the two children in hand; they are all dressed up to go out.

"Where are you going?" he shouts in gross contempt. The little mother looks up with wells of tears starting from her road map eyes.

"It's Sunday, sir, and I thought I'd take the children to church," she says.

"What do you have to take them to church for," the critic roars, *"I'm* here!"

CHAPTER 19

You're in Analysis?

One of the imaginary characters who people our program is our "psycho" analyst Dr. Kology. Dr. Sy Kology is what we call a "saver," in that his appearance in any routine assures acceptance. We are certain that when I do the voice of the old know-it-all, and Finch begins to interview him, we will be able to ad-lib acceptable material. Part of the reason is that the psychologist and the psychiatrist are familiar subjects for satire. Many of our contemporaries have trod the path of better things for better living through head shrinking. However, as we all know, analysis is not without its price.

We retain the utmost respect for real doctors and we maintain a collection of framed, autographed pictures of Dr. B. Casey, Dr. Suess, and Dr. Cronkite. We also have an autographed toothbrush from Dr. West.

For those who will not or cannot avail themselves of psychoanalysis, Klavan and Finch created Dr. Kology, a graduate of the University of Jackson Heights, which we also created. The doctor is the recipient of the Ph D degree for his thesis, "Is Insanity an End in Itself?"

It seems appropriate to include in this volume, a transcript of an address made by the eminent Klavan and Finch consultant at the Department of Tropical Aches and Pains, the University of Miami Beach Medical School:

An address by Dr. S. Kology Ph D, variously entitled:
NEUROTIC, PSYCHOTIC, WHAT'S THE DIFFERENCE IF
IT DON'T SHOW?

The speaker:
Dr. Kology was born in Oslo, Sweden, the son of an itinerant coutourier. The father, always under the impression that Oslo was in Norway, felt out of place, and disappeared into the midnight sun. This left young Sy to support his family which consisted of a wicked stepmother, two half-sisters (which made one whole sister) and a wayward brother. The brother, the villagers said, was "well-fixed" which reassured Sy until he found out what a "fix" was.
Sy abandoned this motley crew while he was still small enough to stow away on a troop transport, posing as a duffle bag. He arrived in America and attended P.S. 62.
In 1961 he was awarded two tickets to "The Price Is Right."

My fellow PhD's:
I am overjoyed to be here in Miami Beach to speak to you because of the fact that I was invited. I am reminded

always of the patient I had who became a criminal. He used to collect the placards that the FBI posted in the post office with his picture on them. My diagnosis of the trouble was easy: he simply needed to feel wanted.

I also knew a baker who wanted to feel kneaded, but that is another case history which I hope to make into a book and sell to the movies.

I am, as you know, the only staff psychologist on a morning radio show. There are psychologists on television answering questions for ladies and like that, usually people like Dr. Joyce Brothers. I would thank you not to insult Dr. Brothers because she may be somebody's mothers or sisters.

I have been invited here to explain what it is that psychologists do not do, that they should do to increase revenue and get ahead with head shrinking. I believe that psychology has to be modernized. You may remember that I originated the mobile couch, a motorized sofa which enabled the analyst to travel quickly from one place to another. With a motorized couch and a level floor, I have been able to sweep through an entire business office cutting ten minutes off each hour. This enables me to give a group-fare plan. I have a motorized couch with white sidewalls available for Park Avenue and other hoity-toity hot beds of neuroses. Furthermore, I also provide phrenology maps and Big-Little books in the glove compartment of my couch for patients who just don't feel like talking. I also have an eject couch for patients who hate goodbyes. I like to mention my double couch for people who hate to do things alone.

In 1963, I became the first analyst to give out plaid stamps. I also project movies on the ceiling for people who are well but have no place to go for an hour. As you can see, innovations are nothing new to me.

Today, I come to you bearing a simple message: Keep your mind off your mind. From my sojourns into the mind I have learned this: The only thing to fear is the fear of being afraid of being afraid. Don't worry about strangers, keep your eye on your best friend.

August is the best time of the year for me, knock wood. All of the other analysts in the big cities are on vacation in August. That is why I do not go on vacation in August, but I hide waiting to help some needy patient. Whenever I spot anybody's patient, I whisper, "Psst, how about a session before your doctor comes back?"

If they show any interest I whip out my folding army cot and make a fast twenty dollars. The only trouble with this kind of analysis is that you have to learn to be a good lookout as well as a good listener. I must admit that I was discovered by a policeman one day analyzing a new patient near Radio City. I was forced to fold up the patient in the army cot and throw him into a subway entrance. That patient's story began in a little house in Akron, Ohio, and ended up in an express station at Wall Street. I guess I didn't help him too much. Because of the army cot, today he still thinks he's a bivouac.

So you see, doctors in the head dodge, the only thing is not to think about what you're thinking about, but just think. And just think what that can mean.

Part of the analyst's problem is that he is surrounded

by people who think they are going mad. Going crazy is so easy to do, we all know, that if you have to think about it, you must be out of your mind. With the way traffic is these days, it's easier to go out of your mind than to go home. The main problem with this modern world is that there are so many restrictions on all of us that we are all afraid to do what we really want to do. If you feel that you really want to go crazy; then do so to preserve your sanity. In this, as always, we can learn from the young. If you ask most teenagers today what they think of normality, they will answer, "Crazy!"

The Cornell University Graduate School made a test in New York in which they discovered that four out of five people walking around were partially insane. The explanation is perfectly obvious. Those four people were half-crazy trying to figure out what was wrong with that other guy.

In summation, I would like to answer some of the questions that have come through the transom over my desk, and over the phone in thinly disguised voices.

The first question is from a lady or a laddy in Provincetown, Mass.: Why is there so much homosexuality these days?

My answer is that the fault probably lies with Dr. Freud and his followers, many of whom were Jung at heart. A generation ago, if a man passed forty and was unmarried, he was a proud bachelor. Today he is a latent homosexual. He is also older. But we must take these early insights into consideration. If it were left to Freud, Cinderella would still be sharing pumpkin seeds with those mice while she turned her Fairy Godmother over to the vice squad.

The second question is from a gentleman on the island of Elba: "What do you call someone with a superiority complex?"

Lucky.

Question from a German doctor who plays piano music in the jungles of Africa: "If a medicine were discovered that would cure all mental problems, what would the psychologists do?"

Become druggists.

From a former première of France: "Isn't it true that all psychologists and psychiatrists enter the work because they have some problem in their own personality make-up?"

Decidedly not. I myself have never had a problem in my life that was not easily solved. Because of this sureness of myself, many people are insanely jealous of me. Although it does not bother me, I am fully aware that someone is always trying to kill me.

I should like to leave you with this final thought: *Honi soit qui mal y pense*. Translated this means, "Money isn't everything, but since you can't have everything—take the money."

CHAPTER 20

No Contest

Once upon a time, a small radio station decided to run a contest for charitable purposes. The idea was that listeners would attempt to guess the identity of a person whose voice had been recorded. Every night during the contest, the announcer would call one of the people who had sent in a contribution, along with his or her telephone number.

The "mystery" voice was a lady, let us call her—shhh —Mrs. Donner, whose altruism and civic virtue were well known in the community but whose voice and countenance were not.

It was all that the little radio station could do to get together the $5000 pile of prizes. After six weeks, if no one had guessed the identity of the woman whose voice it was, even after the clues which were to be doled out, the entire $5000 was to be donated to the charity.

There was much promotion of the contest in advance. After the first program was on the air, everyone became sickeningly tense as the young announcer, Gene Klavan, picked up the phone to make the first call. There was worry that he would botch the detail somehow and confuse or disgruntle the people he was calling. Inasmuch as fifteen minutes a night had been set aside for a six-week period, it was incumbent upon Klavan to handle the program so that suspense would build and "play" interestingly.

The first number he dialed rang for an interminable time. *Someone* must be home, he thought; after all, they had sent their number in. Was anyone going to answer?

Finally, the sparrowlike voice of a little old lady came through in distinct contrast to the excited tones of the announcer. The brief interview began. Then the record of the mystery lady's voice was played and the suspense heightened, starting to build.

"Do you know who she is?" Klavan asked in high excitement.

"Oh yes," the lady replied calmly, "it's Mrs. Donner." And it was, of course, Mrs. Donner. And that was the end of the contest.

For the next six weeks, the audience—or what was left of it—heard a fifteen-minute transcribed program, which had been prepared by the Veterans Administration.

Carefully planned, each detail scrupulously attended to, rehearsed on paper a dozen times, handled by pros, each loophole plugged, the contest was over almost before it was begun. And that is the way contests go, even when they are honest.

We have been involved with contests and promotional competitions for years. Ultimately, we came to advocate the fix. At least then we are sure that the program will be all right. Unhappily, because of their short sighted judgment and sloppy thinking, our superiors have refused to concede that Klavan and Finch's wrong way is the right way. Their childlike honesty has always kept us from enjoying the great rewards which we like to feel are wrongfully ours. They remain consistently uncooperative, despite the fact that we have offered to split the take with them each time.

Nevertheless, we have run unusual contests. From the experience, we have formulated the Klavan and Finch Law of Contest Conducting. We welcome contributions to the theory, but entering would be largely futile, inasmuch as we know the law to be uncontestable. In the case of duplicate entries, judges will be awarded.

The Klavan and Finch Law of Contest Conducting begins, quite seriously, with the following truth: "Response to contests is inversely proportional to the size of the prize."

In other words, the bigger the prize, the fewer entries. How come? If you consider the psychology behind this[1] it is probable that when prizes become so large that they become an almost incomprehensible big deal, people simply do not believe it possible that they can win. They also seem to feel that an avalanche of entries will swamp their entry, leaving them no chance at all. I understand this because I am one of them. Because I cannot find the fortune in a fortune cookie, it is inconceivable to me that anyone could win a car or a boat. But it is conceivable that one would win a power mower or a transistor radio.

Two or three years ago, New York had a Siberian win-

[1] See *Consider the Psychology Behind This,* by Dr. S. Chology, Roarschock House, N.Y., N.Y., 1953, .93¢, 42 pages.

ter. Every new day was an excursion into mountains of
snow and treacherous ice. There were headaches and back-
aches everywhere. Each snow shovel and power shovel in
the area was quickly sought out and purchased. Somehow
or other, we located what was apparently the last power
shovel in the northeastern part of the United States. The
cost was approximately $80. We offered the shovel on the
air as a giveaway. All the listener had to do was to send
in a card with his name and address and we would pull
one out of a hat. We ran the announcement for three days
—and received more than 30,000 cards. There was no
second prize, there were no runners-up—just one lone snow
thrower. This was a prize people could fathom and it was
sort of fun to try to win it.

We have, on the other hand, run prizes where the giveaway was a trip around the world, or a mink coat, and we
have gotten nothing like a comparative response. Ironically,
the people who enter those contests have a better chance to
win, given the mathematical probabilities, than those trying to win the snow thrower.

The second rule of the K & F contest theorem: Keep it
simple. If you complicate a contest with a great many
provisos and conditions, you lower the response. You can
get an immense return if you merely ask for cards with
names and addresses. But if you ask your listeners to qual-
ify their entries by naming their reasons why the world will
end, or their brief description, in twenty-five words or less,
of the theory of relativity, you will not hear from anyone
but your relatives and they are, of course, ineligible. Relatively speaking.

It is our policy, incidentally, to have nothing to do with the judging or selection of winners. We hate losing friends.

Some contests are run purely for the sake of getting people to listen—forcing them, if you will. When one New York radio station hid $1000 in the city and gave out clues to the location, the audience increased two or threefold. People talked about it all over town. Some youngsters gave up rock and roll and fast living to concentrate on finding the money instead. There were wild scenes on the street. But oddly enough, after the contest was over, the station's ratings dropped off as rapidly as they had increased. Why didn't the station keep dropping thousand-dollar bills until they had gained all the listeners in town? One reason is that we and other stations were sabotaging their efforts by giving out the clues right after they gave them on the air. This might not have been cricket, but it did make for a cleaner New York, not having all that money lying around.

The third rule is: The timing must be right. Timing, that ever-important word in all show business, is extremely important in contests. An alert program director, who is no longer with us, suggested to us that we run a contest to name the first American earth satellite. This makes a good deal of sense, viewed from the present time. But to put the suggestion in proper perspective, it should be said that the suggestion was made at a time before there was *any* satellite in the sky. The United States was going to attempt launching the Vanguard Project satellite in about six months. There was no Russian satellite and Sputnik was only the sound that a car makes starting on a cold morning. Finch and I suggested that since the public apparently knew as much as we did about satellites, perhaps we had better bone up on the situation and tell the audience about it before starting the contest. We were whisked away to Washington where we inspected the Navy Department's progress, saw the satellite, picked up as much unclassified material as possible, and then were whiskeyed back to New York. As a clincher in the contest, to help the public get the concept of satellites, we decided to offer as a first prize, a trip around the world. By conventional means.

In retrospect, the contest, with its mammoth first prize, which included spending money, etc., and the second prize of a new station wagon, looked provocative and attention-getting. There was only one hitch—the timing.

The public was unconcerned with rockets and satellites at the time. We had to explain too much about the space program. The contest was hardly the flaming success it should have been. In contrast to what its potential seemed to be, the response was negligible. The winning name, Pioneer, was selected and the happy winners received their prizes while the rest of us sat around commiserated at the unhappy blow fate had dealt us from under the deck. Then, to rub it in, the Russians launched Sputnik I. If we had attempted to get our contest off the ground the next day, with the attendant publicity, it would have been one of the greatest radio coups of all time. As it was, everybody thought we were just coup coup. As Mother always said, if you have to explain 'em, they're no good.

But of all these rules, the simplicity thought is the most important. People do not have time to get themselves involved in shenanigans of all sorts just to have an outside chance, and a long shot at the shadow of a hope of winning. We once ran what we thought was an appealing contest, called Hooky Day. The idea of this little extravaganza was that listeners were to write on a card, their names and the names of their employer. If we selected a listener's card, that lucky person was to be allowed a day off by the management of his company—and Klavan and Finch would give that company a free commercial in return for the favor.

In other words, our listeners could play hooky if we payed off the boss. As we search the grim and dusty past of contests, it is not surprising that the companies loved the idea. But the employees were not as entranced. After all, when the employee returned, he still had the same amount of work to do even though his boss now had benefited by a $180 commercial. In addition, the entrant would have had to ask the boss's permission to participate in the first place—and many hesitated to enter because they didn't want to ask the permission of The Chief.

Nevertheless, it was a reasonably successful contest, especially in that it was copied by radio stations all over the country. It seemed like a good idea at the time and I wish we had thought of it, but the truth is that we bought it from an unfrocked record plugger.

At one point, we gave away a paper bag full of subway tokens. The station gave away a full house, lot, and boat at a seashore resort in another contest. These were hugely successful in talk value. But neither paralleled the "Doodli Boop" contest for fun and simplicity.

"Doodli Boop" was a Christmas novelty record which we played frequently. After putting it on the air one time, we asked ingenuously, "I wonder what a Doodli Boop is?" Answers poured in from the audience, so we decided to make a contest of it. The first prize was a mink coat, a color television set, hundreds of dollars worth of toys, watches, etc.

When the contest was over, we were allowed to sit in the room while the judges, including the president of a prominent advertising agency, and the singer, Patti Page, thought carefully as they examined the entries. Many of the entries which made their way into the finals were tremendously creative, the products of imaginative minds. There were beautiful paintings in oils and water colors, books completely written, illustrated and bound; artefact and sculpted figurines, humorous drawings and clever treatises—all telling us what a Doodli Boop really was.

The judges astounded us by selecting a simple little poem with innocent drawings. They said they were impressed with its sincerity and directness. Over a hundred other finalists, they picked an entry by a lady in New Jersey whose effort comprised only one page.

At this point, we all trooped into a van and went singing over the George Washington Bridge to deliver the loot to the lucky lady. We were more than excited, anticipating her joy and surprise. She was to be showered with treasures. And after all, this was a local contest, one program, from an independent station, and clearly a nice victory for a nice lady.

When we arrived at the winner's home and delivered

the prizes, we prepared to tape record a statement. There was something puzzling about the winner and we were confounded by her composure.

"Well, aren't you excited over winning a beautiful mink coat and the TV and all?" Finch asked, excitement charging his mellifluous tones.

"Not really, but I will be happy to wear the coat out to California."

"Oh," Finch said, "you're going to California?"

"Yes. I won a trip for my husband and myself."

"You've won," Finch said, "other contests?" Disappointment dripped from his every word.

"I win them all the time," she smiled, as she tried on a watch or two and helped us unload the truck.

And so she had. I am sure she still goes on winning. This lovely New Jersey housewife runs a charming house, has a well-adjusted family, and the fortunate and unusual talent of being a perennial contest winner. She is one of those people who have a knack for knowing what is expected of contests and of being able to fulfill the requirements.

This is our final word on contests, at least for this volume. Our interest in them has flagged somewhat, especially because employees of the station and their families are not eligible. But even if we were, there would be little use in trying. A talent for winning contests is as fortunate and unusual as a talent for making money. This is the sort of gift which is apparently handed down from your parents; I do not think it can be learned. According to most people, it cannot be hereditary because it is a recessive gene. And frankly, so am I.

CHAPTER 21

The Old College Try

Though modern psychiatry has taught us that an alma mater is just a mother-substitute, there is a fascination with college that we never lose even though college days are now the property of someone else. We never lose the excitement or challenge that we felt as we entered the gates, or fail to feel the tear run down as we left, expelled. Gone forever is the carefree moment of youth, gone is the heady broth of knowledge, gone is the old man's dough, and now the GI Bill is a goner too.

Unfortunately, some of the things that reminded us about those days are gone too: the movies about college life have all but disappeared.

Everyone remembers the movies when Peter Lawford was the exchange student from England, in love with June Allyson or Judy Garland: while Desi Arnaz the rich, spoiled kid tried to steal both girls away.

And who can disassociate himself from the tears when Walter Pidgeon, as the young economics prof, was forced to flunk Lucille Ball out in *Girls and Money Don't Mix*.

Most of the pictures of those days were musicals with vast production numbers. The entire assemblage would do the finale, streaming out of Dorm C, led by Ann Sothern and Martha Raye. The dean, always played alternately by Lewis Stone or Lionel Barrymore, eventually agrees not to flunk Sonny Tufts in his finals so that Sonny can play in the game on Saturday and bring the championship back to State. And, if memory serves, Sonny always did it— with a broken leg and internal injuries. There is also the undercurrent of danger that the South will win the war— but perhaps that is another series of pictures.

We believe, and this is one of the inside tips with which this book is replete, that it is time for a new series of musicals about college life. Having finished such a script, we submitted it to major stars and large motion picture companies. So far, we are unhappy to report, the script has come back with what we consider unreasonable requests and untenable recommendations.

If you feel as enthusiastic as we do, and can find the backing, here is a completely workable script for a modern-day collegiate motion picture musical:

ALL AMERICAN PRODUCTIONS
Kyoto, Japan
PRESENTS
GO STATE GO

(The picture opens with a panoramic view of School-ville, U.S.A., a small but lovely college town that shows evidences of just having recovered from a student riot. It is a typical Midwestern school and the campus is dominated by the administration building from whence the brutal but efficient campus police can keep an eye on the politically oriented frosh. Torn posters appear everywhere; DOWN WITH THE PEACE CORPS, STUDENTS GO HOME, BETTER READ THAN ILLITERATE, THE JOHN BIRCH SOCIETY AIN'T NOBODY'S FRIEND.

The camera moves quickly through the town, past the Plaid Stamp Redemption Center, the expresso houses, down the main street past the NCAA, the NAACP, the ROTC, and the small loan office.

It is fall and the campus is alive with color: pinks, reds, bluenoses, black shirts, and neutrals . . . As we approach the student activities building, the first notes of the opening number come cascading out of the band practice room. Coeds sitting on the steps turn away from boy students busily engaged in a study of comparative anatomy, and all sing:)

(Happily, joyously, but martially)

HOORAY FOR SCHOOL

Hooray for school; huzzah for education
For things like that—and love.
Don't be a fool, you learn an occupation.
To beat the Russkis with our satellites above.

We're real sincere and fully integrated
And some have found a mate.
What taxes pay for is appreciated
And so is Federal aid—
At least until we overthrow the State!

(Then ensues a brief dance number in which the girls rip off their sweaters, revealing brief coveralls which are symbolic of their spirit of work and devotion to duty. They dance an interpretive number, signifying disenchantment with the flabby American. The boys have donned some identifying piece of insignia of the armies of the world thereby implying one-worldness and they move into a musical series of calisthenics. The dance number ends with a locomotive cheer, led by a coed with a baby in her arms:)

> Rabbety ribbety, sibbety, crease
> Ban the bomb and pray for peace!
> Siggitey, saggety, habbety hay,
> Kill any bastard who gets in your way!
> Yeaah peace! Ray love!
> Humanity! humanity! Bye Bye Bye!

(For the first time, we meet the stars of our movie. All students rush off to a protest rally, waving beakers of strontium 90, except a beautiful blonde, Sally Middleton. Sally is an economics major who is minoring in Free Fall Parachuting from under 2000 feet. She is joined by Wright Wing who appears from behind a bush. Wright is the right halfback of the football team. He tries to kiss her, but she pulls away.)

SALLY: Don't you see—I'm the only girl in the freshman class who's not married. How can I ever finish college like this? I'd be the laughingstock of State.

WRIGHT: Aw, come on, you know that marriage is out of the question and also out of the answer. I have my studies, my membership in the Young Americans for Restoration

of the Goldwater Standard. And don't forget my obligation
to the team—they're paying my way, you know.

(*He sings plaintively:*)

WHY CAN'T WE GO ON THIS WAY FOREVER?
Why can't we go on this way forever?
Don't let marriage tear our love apart,
Easters in Fort Lauderdale with all the college sprites
Who cares what the *Reader's Digest* writes

Marriage was never made for single people
Let's not taint a love like ours with hate
Let's just live together here, in paradise forever here
At least until we graduate.

(The obvious intelligence of this sentimentality moves
Sally to tears and she runs off to sewing class, leaving
Wright morosely bouncing a football off the statue of the
university's founder, Andy Hardy.

Camera cuts to the second leads. We see, outside his
fraternity house, Reds Left, the left end of the football
squad. With the pittance that he makes sewing little ham-
mers and sickles on the tassles for the flags for the local
chapter of the Young Leftwingers of America, he is paying his way through college. He is majoring in the psychology of crowds. Reds looks around and sees Sally crying. He lopes over to her and hands her his bandanna.)

REDS: Why are you crying, Sally?

SALLY: I'll tell you.

REDS: Yes, tell me why you are crying.

SALLY: I'll tell you why I'm crying. Daddy's given me an ultimatum.

REDS: An imperialistic gambit! The rotten American legionnaire!

SALLY: Daddy's in the VFW, but I love you for your sentimentality and understanding. Daddy says I must get married by June or just not to bother coming home. If I don't marry soon, he's going to take away my membership in the Columbia Record of the Month Club, and you know what that means to a teenage girl!

(Reds is suddenly cold. He looks away to the faroff steppes of Pennsylvania.)

REDS: I'd marry you in a moment, Sally, if I believed in marriage. But you know my ideals of free love and a summer camp for accountants. I would hate myself for being a party to any wedding party.

(Now, we have the gist of the conflict. Not only will tall successful wingback, Wright Wing not marry her, neither will tall brooding left end, Reds Left. At this down moment of the story, we introduce the comic relief, little Prep Ayers, the only pre-med on the campus. Prep is the laughingstock of all the male students, not only because he is only five foot eleven, 192 pounds, and therefore not football material, but because he is a pre-med, with eight years of college, two years of internship, years of residency to go before he is able to make big money. He is a ridiculous fellow to all and he sings his introductory number:)

MINE SON, THE DOCTOR

Why am I going through this aggravation?
Why do I need an education?

Why should I spend time and money this way,
Just so I can hear my father say:
(*Chorus*)
Mine son, the doctor; mine son, the doctor.
How about mine son, the building controctor
How about mine son, the lawyer or octor.
How about mine son, the garbage colloctor
No it's gotta be, mine son, the doctor.

A coach of socctor, an interloctur
Or the pilot of a helicoctor
How about mine son the TV diroctor.
How about mine son, the plumbing connoctor
How about mine son, the story concoctor—

No, they won't be happy till I'm thru
That's my mother and father, the doctors, too!

(Entire chorus of students appears and joins in a dance to exemplify the futility of graduate school education over the fast buck. The dance comes to a swift finale, when the students, revealing that the dancing tunics they wear are made from *The Wall Street Journal*.)

(Prep Ayers turns to speak to Sally. He tells her he wants to marry her because he believes in true love and fidelity. All of the students laugh at this appreciatively until an unattractive but charming comedienne, Herta Call, steps out of the crowd and swears undying love to Prep. She gets one of the biggest laughs by holding out a darling baby and sobbing:

HERTA: Doesn't our biology experiment mean anything to you?

(The scene dissolves.

It is Friday night, at the riot before the football game. The crowd begins to become unruly, angry snarls and jeers emanating from the dissident political elements. A small group of students—Sally, Prep Ayers, Herta Call and the baby—stand off to one side, looking on, but not participating. Sally speaks:)

SALLY: Oh how will we ever win the big game tomorrow if the team and all are expending their energy having fun at the riots?

PREP: Yes, it's terrible to be a member of a minority group, the plain everyday ordinary Americans. Needn't we middle-of-the-roaders be heard from too?

(The scene is suddenly electrified by the arrival of the president of the university, Skeets Schweitzer, who quiets the riot by waving a colorfully painted, humorously lettered tear gas dispenser. From the center of the milling crowd, steps the center of the football team, Flip Median. He approaches the president of the school.)

FLIP: Why do you have to come down here for and stop all the fun. If the boys want to uncork a little riot, what's it to you?

SCHWEITZER: (*Putting his hand on Flip's shoulder pads*) How come you want all this violence to continue?

FLIP: Because I'm a graduate of a permissive school; a son of permissive parents. I believe that the trouble with America today is that nobody listens to the youth. You won't listen, my parents won't listen. Nobody will listen!

SCHWEITZER: What? I'm awfully sorry. I wasn't listening.

SALLY: (*Suddenly interested*) You spoke good, Flip. Are you married?

FLIP: Not necessarily. What did you have in mind?

SALLY: Listening to Columbia Records of the Month together forever. But you needn't answer until the last reel if you don't want to.

(*Sally shyly bursts into song:*)

I NEED A MAN

I need a man, I need a man, I need a man
To dominate, to subjugate
To run my errands and capitulate
To slave away while I just vegetate,
I need a man.

I need a man, I need a man, I need a man
To give to me, security.
And take care of my family
So they can live along with me
In luxury—
I need a man
To love!

(Flip responds to this touching little plea by telling Sally his point-of-view.)

FLIP: I'm more than just the center of the team. I'm our youth against their youth. I'm the future of yesterday and the past of tomorrow and visa versa.

SALLY: (*Impressed*) And you've got great legs.

FLIP: A man needs a wife in today's complex life. That also rhymes. Sally, will you marry me?

SALLY: Oh yes, Flip. When?

(Flip enfolds her in his arms carefully so as not to disarrange his shoulder pads.)

FLIP: As soon as I can get my divorce.

SALLY: But they'll bust you from the team for breaking training. You know the rules against getting a divorce during the season.

(She starts to sniffle; he gives her reassurance and an antihistamine.)

FLIP: Learning is more important today than sports. You can't plug the missile gap with the *Look* Magazine All-American Awards. If they throw me out of school, I'll do what all the college kids are doing today.

SALLY: (*with feeling*) What?

FLIP: I'll become a combination sick-comedian and folk singer.

(They fall into each other's arms and drop to the campus. The camera discreetly pans up to the sky and the scene fades out.)

Final scene: Graduation Day. Flip is at the center of the auditorium stage with Sally, their three children and her father. Sally's father is presenting her with a renewal in the Columbia Record of the Month Club. Prep is also there, now happily married to Flip's first wife. He has given up the ridiculous notion of going to medical school and is about to enter the wholesale ice cream business. Herta Call, the comedienne, has married the president of the university, Skeets Schweitzer, who was really the father of her biology experiment in the first place. Reds Left and

Wright Wing are seen picketing the entire graduation as
Un-American.

The entire cast sings the finale:

ALL FOR ONE AND ONE FOR ALL

Everybody wants to join the Peace Corps,
It's the place where everybody serves.
It's the one corps, the sun and fun corps
And it's better than fighting the draft or the reserves.

Whether it's teaching guitar or crop rotation
We will go wherever they insist.
We'll show each dirty gook and backward nation
That the ugly American doesn't really exist.

All together now for Uncle Sammy
Here's a duty we cannot shirk.
Though the hours are long, the pay is not—
      There's quicksand and the jungle rot,
It's better than going out to work!

THE END

CHAPTER 22

I Didn't Raise My Voice to Be a Sermon

One of the sneaky things about radio is its refusal to die. By all odds, it should have perished after the near-fatal attack of television it suffered in 1948 or so. Convulsions were evident, the death rattles were there. Many of the creative people were clamoring for their last rights (so they could run off and sell them to TV). What had been a massive, healthy audience paled to a deathly shadow, leaving radio sick and delirious, talking to itself at night. Many station owners, fearful of being caught with a corpse, sold their stations at prices far below their full value. This allowed the entry of shortsighted people interested only in the horsetrading of broadcast licenses for capital gains. Radio became a good investment for people who were interested not in radio but in the investment. You could build up a station's ratings, and sell it to somebody else who would try to sell it to somebody else. The problem became one of building up the ratings. And when the ratings were high, you could attempt to sell advertising or you could attempt to sell the station to somebody who would attempt to sell advertising. The radio business was such a whirlpool in the middle fifties that you never had to be nice to the boss because neither you nor he probably would be there the next day anyhow.

People interested in the quick buck were not interested in ideas or paying for long-term, audience-getting performers. Performers were not interested in appearing in a second-rate medium. The networks, concentrating their abilities and money on television, had no time for development of the word or imagination and began diminishing their service until the radio network became little more than an audible news wire. Then, somebody, though nobody will take the rap for this one, invented the "formula." The formula was a system for building up ratings quickly (and then selling the station's time to advertisers or the station itself to a new operator). It was an almost perfect system of instant money. The station had only to throw on forty records all day long—the so called "Top Forty"— and newscasts which were frenetic, loud, and frequent.

An important aspect embodied in the formula operation was giving the listener the impression that something big was going to happen any minute. The listener becomes afraid to turn off the station because he has the gnawing feeling that they knew something that he didn't. If he could only hold on long enough, he, too, would get the inside scoop.

What the station people knew that the listener didn't was that they didn't know anything special either. They only had to give the impression that they did. When there was real news, worthy of a bulletin, they screamed! When there was no bulletin material, they often made one up out of information that barely deserved mention. It was not uncommon to hear bulletins which literally translated really said: "Bulletin, bulletin, bulletin! A tragic five-car accident was narrowly averted when five cars on Chestnut Street and Broad Avenue did not collide this afternoon! Stay tuned to 'Action Central' for more news. You'll hear it first and loudest here! Hear! Hear! Hear!" Those who eventually became attracted to this kind of radio were the young people because it promised them something new and exciting. Formula radio with its frequently unpolished, often downright bad, music offered the teenagers something that was exclusively theirs and not, like television, a property to be shared with grownups. This soon became evident to the advertising agencies as well because this kind of radio was beginning to be supported by cigarettes, cola drinks, and acne cure commercials.

New York was the last to know. Formula radio stayed away from New York for a long time—until it proved itself outside mecca. Then, with a cowardly kind of courage it was injected into the main stream. Ratings soared momentarily until other stations picked up the formula. Then the ratings Ping-ponged over to the new stations. Within a short while, if you wanted to know which station was number one in the rating books, you had to call in the late afternoon of each day for the final score. Finch and I had our little arguments about how we were to handle the influx of this kind of music and programing. I urged adding to our music schedule the best of the new rock and roll. He fought against it. I felt that you had to be apprised of what was going on in the entertainment world and let the audience hear the best of the new music and then decide. Finch said that there was no best of the new music; it was all bad. Our producer, Mike Apicella, said he had a headache. The station manager said that he knew nothing and was prepared to back this up. And Gimbels said that they would not be undersold.

After heated discussion, because it was winter, we decided to compromise and do the best thing. It was the worst thing we could do. We tried to pick out the best of the real rock and roll music and play a record or two a morning. Nothing jarring; nothing ear-splitting. We just played a record of some nice teenagers singing some unintelligible lyrics about a teenage revolt.

At least, all of the records we listened to were revolting teenagers. As you must surmise by now, a compromise of this kind is the worst compromise. The youngsters didn't listen to us anyhow. And those people twenty years or older didn't want that kind of trouble in the morning. I can honestly tell you that one bad record, in the morning, can drive more listeners away than ten loud commercials. Unfortunately, the management of the station agreed with the principle of trying to be all things to all people and advocated the insertion of a few rocking records throughout the broadcast day and night. It had the stimulating effect of an injection of an air bubble into the bloodstream. We were quick to recognize the mistake and yanked out records that were not professional nor entertaining. Now we play everything from progressive jazz and symphony through down-home country and gag records—but they have to be good. Our producer still has a headache but now it's only because he's too vain to wear bifocals. Luckily, while we were going through the throes of decision, the other stations were doing the same sort of soul-searching. For a brief time you could not tell what you were listening to or whether you were going to be listening to the same thing the next day on the same station. And then suddenly, the air cleared and a new and startling fact became clear to everyone, except perhaps the listeners. All radio stations were formula stations, but the formulas were different. There was an all-talk formula, or an all-music formula with no talk; there was a pure rock and roll formula; there was a "personality" formula with personalities and good music; there was a long-hair formula; and there were still the Dr. Jekyll-Mr. Hyde stations—a mishmash of good and bad. Banished forever from the mass-appeal radio stations were the dramatic shows, the soap operas, the children's shows, the variety shows, the really exciting panel and discussion shows, and the mystery stories. These were, for the most part, ceded to television. Some shows of this sort remain on isolated radio stations which have not seen the "green" light. There are still good performers on radio throughout the country. Unfortunately for our sense of security, there are people in cities other than New York and Los Angeles who could move into the major markets in a minute and be immensely successful. Fortunately for us, with the change in status of radio, has come a change of status of the people on the air. Whereas at one time, the ambitious performer always started outside the major cities and ended up seeking the elusive New York big money, he now finds that certain cities offer good money and less expensive living. Apparently, La Vita can be Dolce elsewhere.

Radio will not die. It has had its chance; now whether it likes it or not it is going to have to live. There is too much of a job to be done by the little box, a job that television can never do, nor can publications. The recent rash of talk records, comedy records, horror records, and great readings has proved that the spoken word or the spoken variation of the written word is important to people and can make them happier. With high fidelity, multiplex, and Lord knows what next there is a future for the uses of radio which we cannot even begin to visualize. But it will take a great deal of thought and respect for both the medium and the audience to make it in the competitive days ahead.

The quick-buck boys and the hacks are going to find it increasingly difficult to milk the product. The government, which has recently seen fit to discover that radio is still kicking around, will take a more qualitative interest in seeing who owns the stations and what is being done with them. For radio, the next decade promises to be a far more stimulating one than the last fear-bitten one. In conclusion, let us ask then, not what you will do for radio but what radio will do for you. That is a *great* line and I'm wondering why nobody ever thought of it before.

CHAPTER 23

A Funny Thing Happened on the Way to the Studio?

Anyone who has ever tried to be humorous on a topical subject, runs the risk of being forced out of business by a change of attitudes as well as events. Ours is the daily problem of watching the news to make sure that what was attackable by humor the previous day is still in bounds. For example, we have survived the daily flow of news and the daily needling we do to that news by the simple expedient of fighting with each other.

Of course, the easiest way to survive in the humor department is not to comment on anything that is at all provocative. This safe, sure technique will not get you into any trouble; but on the other hand, it will render you about as fascinating as a dollop of day-old cottage cheese. We believe in stirring up a little trouble every so often and we believe that the audience enjoys it as well. It is difficult not to step on someone's toes in the course of such activities but we have to do what we believe is right even if we are wrong.

The world itself has changed since our association in 1952. In our merry pace to keep up with a world that is snake-hipping itself into oblivion, we have created our own never-never land of radio absurdity. In an attempt to understand our own twisted thinking, we have ended up with four hours of service, disservice, and commentary which can lead to nothing but ten o'clock.

It just isn't like the good old days when there were just the dirty Nazis and the nasty Communists to hate. It's an infinitely more complex world and you can't tell the good guys from the bad guys any more for sure. Or at least for long. For example, take Cuba, if someone doesn't take it before you do. America didn't like Batista and his form of government for our neighbor to the south. On the other hand, when Batista was succeeded by Castro, it didn't take too long before we Americans realized that by our action or inaction we had bought ourselves another bucket of worms.

We therefore made some kind of an attempt to conciliate our relationship with Castro and convince him that we had the better life to offer. Simultaneously, the Russian Reds who were really not our friends at all, were trying to sell him the same story. Also simultaneously, the Chinese Reds, whom we had been insisting for years were really not there at all, were selling him the idea that their way of life was it.

At the same time, we knew that the Russian Reds and the Chinese Reds (who really didn't exist) although friendly, actually hated each other, didn't we? And didn't they?

The Canadians, our friends, continued to deal with the Cubans and the Red Chinese who were not our friends, if they existed at all. We didn't like the fact that our friends were friendly with our non-friends. The Canadians, our friends, didn't like us, their friends, telling them what to do already.

Then an occurrence took place that tended to simplify the situation. At the height of the major Cuban crisis over those Russian missile bases, the Red Chinese overran the lands of their good neighbor to the south, India.

The Russians, with whom we were negotiating to prevent a really big one, those same Russians and ourselves both sent arms to India, a neutral nation engaged in a war with its ally, Red China.

In the midst of this entanglement of alliances, the City of New York went a long way toward easing the situation by preparing for another international holocaust, the World's Fair of 1964.

I guess it becomes more and more evident that it is difficult to make jokes that ricochet off of current events. So rapid are the changes in the status of what should be the status quo that an event that seemed a source for satire when we leave home becomes an unmentionable subject by the time we hit the air.

Many mornings when we awake and go on, the news is so tense and the world is in such a state of turmoil that we just feel like we have to say *something*. And I suppose I wrote this book for the same reason.